D0924625

BONSAI
with American Trees

BONSAI
with American Trees

MASAKUNI KAWASUMI

Introduction by Kyūzō Murata

Kodansha International Ltd.
Tokyo, New York and San Francisco

Distributed in the United States by Kodansha International/USA
through Harper & Row, Publishers, Inc., 10 East 53rd Street, New
York, New York 10022.

Published by Kodansha International Ltd., 12-21, Otowa 2-chome,
Bunkyo-ku, Tokyo 112 and Kodansha International/USA Ltd., 10 East
53rd Street, New York, New York 10022 and The Hearst Building, 5
Third Street, Suite No. 430, San Francisco, California 94103. Photos on
pages 13-20 copyright © 1975 by Keizō Kaneko; remaining photos and
text copyright © 1975 by Kodansha International Ltd. All rights reserved. Printed in Japan.

LCC 75-10588
ISBN 0-87011-619-3
ISBN 4-7700-1119-9 (in Japan)

First edition, 1975
First paperback edition, 1983
Second printing, 1984

CONTENTS

A LETTER FROM
THE JAPAN BONSAI ASSOCIATION

It is always heartening news for us bonsai enthusiasts to know of a new publication. And especially if the author happens to be not only the leading authority on bonsai in Japan, but also very well informed on bonsai activities in countries abroad.

I am sure that bonsai fans in the United States will regard this publication as a "bible" of the art. It explains in detail what species of trees are appropriate for bonsai in different regions, how they should be taken care of, and, more importantly, he has included a valuable and original section on the tools used for bonsai.

The advancements made in recent years in the techniques of growing bonsai has made it imperative for the cultivator to obtain an accurate grasp of all the new tools available and the proper way of using them. Fifty years ago, all we had were ordinary garden shears until Mr. Kawasumi's father invented the first shears for bonsai. This was followed by other inventions that were devised together with Mr. Murata, who assisted with this book.

Today the author has succeeded his father and he has invented a great variety of improved instruments through practical experimentation. These tools have contributed greatly to the advance and development of the art, and without exaggeration I say that we could not have witnessed progress in bonsai without them.

I am, therefore, fully convinced that readers will now find the art of bonsai much easier as well as more enjoyable.

TEISUKE TAKAHASHI
Vice-President
Japan Bonsai Association

INTRODUCTION

Through meeting and talking to visitors who have come to my nursery over the years, I know that people from all over the world are being increasingly attracted to this Japanese art. Bonsai itself has become a household word internationally. Interest in this ancient and traditional art, which until lately has been confined to our island of Japan, has spread over sea and land and is reaching more and more enthusiasts who learn about it through photographs, magazines, or perhaps during a visit to Japan.

In the United States in particular, bonsai has become a good way to occupy one's leisure time, but beyond this it is also the ideal hobby for those seeking a more spiritual kind of relaxation. What better means of mental and physical satisfaction is there than the careful nurturing of these delicate, beautiful trees that are a perfect echo of nature? And what better reward is there than watching them form and flourish as time passes?

At a glance bonsai seems a relatively simple hobby—after all, trees in the open grow and survive without any care. Though you may like its simplicity for a while, the longer you practice it, the more difficulties you will discover as you continue. This is where this book is so functional and so practical. It deals with all types of problems, whether you are a beginner or someone who wants more detailed information on a specialized technique.

I know that a large number of books have already been written on bonsai, both by Japanese and American enthusiasts, but here is one, which in my opinion, surpasses them all. It is the direct result of Mr. Kawasumi's long, personal experience with and his wide background in the art both in Japan and the United States. He has lived in these regions, including Europe, and is fully aware of the situations prevalent there. He has met and exchanged views with a number of foreign bonsai enthusiasts and collected an enormous amount of data and material, the quintessence of which is included in this volume. To quote the vice-president of the Japan Bonsai Association,

Mr. Kawasumi is "one of the few masters in Japan who is really in touch with the activities of bonsai enthusiasts in the United States and Europe." It is his continuing contact with both worlds that makes this book such an essential addition to your bonsai library.

It is my expectation that this book will reach the hands of many bonsai fans throughout the world, for it is as timely as it is useful.

KYŪZŌ MURATA
February, 1975

AUTHOR'S PREFACE

It may not be simple coincidence that bonsai has developed and flourished in Japan. Our country is blessed by a temperate climate and characterized by natural geographical features ranging from snow-capped mountains to sun-drenched beaches, and a profusion of rivers, lakes, forests, and hills that has produced an abundance and variety of plant life astonishing for a region that is smaller than the state of California.

The four distinct seasons, for which we have been traditionally famed, have helped us to develop an affinity with nature, and through this a great love for nature in all its manifestations. This instinct for nature, if I may call it that, is today increasingly shared by people all over the world, and this small volume is my contribution to this gathering interest.

What is bonsai, you may ask? To followers of the art an answer may not be necessary, but I would like to address beginners who are interested, but not practiced, in the art.

Bonsai is a tree or a shrub raised in a small pot and cultivated in miniature. Ideally, it should possess all the beauty and naturalness of a tree found in its usual environment, even though it is only a fraction of the size. This, however, does not mean that any potted plant is automatically bonsai any more than a plant growing in the same pot for many years can be called bonsai. The difference is that bonsai is grown not for the beauty of the miniature tree alone but is admired and appreciated together with the pot as an aesthetic whole.

In Japan through the centuries we have cultivated a great many bonsai styles ranging from the famed white pine that was first planted four hundred years ago to the Matsudaira miniature bonsai, no larger than a thumb, which has survived for eighty years. Both are classic examples of Japanese bonsai.

In America bonsai is still in its infant stages and you have not had the experience of long years of cultivating bonsai as we have had in Japan. This, I feel, is a great advantage, for just as a pet takes on the disposition of its owner, so bonsai in the United States will reflect the personality of American enthusiasts. When the American personality becomes expressed in bonsai, it will be the turn of American bonsai to go abroad with the ambition of being recognized for both its reputation and its beauty. This, I am sure, will take place in the near future.

I have made my book very explicit both for the beginner and the specialist so that it may be used as a guide by everyone interested in the art. Bonsai, besides being less rigid than the tea ceremony or the flower arrangement, also offers more scope and satisfaction to those willing to experiment. So if you have a few hours to spare a week and a few pots lying around the house, why not try it for yourself. You will enjoy the best of nature from season to season without venturing further than your own house or garden.

It is my very great pleasure to dedicate this book to bonsai enthusiasts everywhere and especially to those I met on my visits to America who showed their genuine appreciation of this Japanese art.

MASAKUNI KAWASUMI
February, 1975

Five-needle Pine, 100 years old (14 in.)

A view of a typical Japanese bonsai nursery

Five-needle Pine, 60 years old (22 in.)

Zelkova, 100 years old (36 in.)

Persimmon, 150 years old (30 in.)

Autumn Cherry, 60 years old (19¼ in.)

Five-needle Pine, 150 years old (24 in.). with *Acorus gramineus* Soland

Sugar Maple, 30 years old (30 in.), with Japanese sweet flags

A display of miniature bonsai. From top left anticlockwise: *Ezo* Spruce,
20 years old (5½ in.); Holly, 18 years old (8 in.); Crab Apple, 18 years old
(7 in.); *Kiyohime* Maple, 10 years old (5 in.); Five-needle Pine, 15 years old
(6 in.) and Japanese sweet flags; Japanese Mountain Maple, 25 years
old (12 in.)

CHAPTER 1

BONSAI
FOR
BEGINNERS

Almost all trees and shrubs native to the United States can be successfully adapted for bonsai, except for a few species of trees with long leaves, which cannot be miniaturized. Some examples of these trees are the long-needle pine (*Pinus palustris* Mill), the loblolly pine (*Pinus taeda* L.) that grows from Virginia to Florida and also in Texas, the Douglas fir (*Pseudotsuga menziesi*) found in the Western states, and the long-leafed willow (*Populus nigra* L.) of the Midwest.

Bonsai, unlike their natural counterpart, can live easily in regions that are not their natural habitat, whether this be in the Arctic or the Temperate Zones. This is one of the great pleasures of the art of bonsai, for it means that trees and plants of faraway regions can be planted and appreciated without traveling.

To beginners in the art, I would advise the cultivation of only those species found in their area, and from there they can gradually experiment with other trees and shrubs that are not native.

TREES AND SHRUBS USED FOR BONSAI

Although the classic bonsai is the Japanese white (five-needle) pine, bonsai enthusiasts in America have introduced a long list of American trees that have been successfully miniaturized. The following species are among the most popular in America.

American Cypress	*Chamaecyparis thyoides* Britt.
Scarlet Maple (Red Maple)	*Acer rubrum* L.
Canadian Hemlock	*Tsuga canadensis* Carr.
Collected American Crab Apple	*Malus sp.*
North American Alberta Spruce	*Picea glauca var.* Albertinia
American Bald Cypress	*Taxodium distichum* Rich
Pitch Pine	*Pinus rigida* Mill
Blaauw's Juniper	*Juniperus chinensis var.* Blaaui
American Juniper	*Juniperus chinensis var.* Foemina
Black Spruce	*Picea brevifolia* Reck
Norwegian Spruce	*Picea abies* Cv.
Montezuma Cypress	*Taxodium mucronatum* Ten.
American Hazelnut	*Corylus americana* Marsh.
Shore Pine (Beach Pine)	*Pinus contorta* Loud.

Lodgepole Pine	*Pinus murrayana*
Swiss Mountain (Mugo) Pine	*Pinus mugo Pumilio*

Because of their straight, short leaves, small buds, and their pleasant shapes, the following species are also excellent for bonsai.

Californian Juniper	*Juniperus california* Carriere
Prostrata Juniper	*Juniperus squamata var. Prostrata*
Golden Cup Oak	*Quercus charysolepis* Liebman
Silver-Blue Atlas Cedar	*Cedrus atlantica var. Glauca*
Pomegranate	*Punica granantum* L.
Chinese Elm	*Ulmus parvifolia* Jacq.
Japanese Maple	*Acer palmatum* Thunb.
Rock Cotoneaster	*Cotoneaster horizontalis* Decne.
All Cryptomeria species	
All Juniper species	
All Pyracantha species	

These are only some of the numerous species of trees and shrubs native to America that are suitable for bonsai. Other available species that you can choose from are: the Japanese black pine, the five-needle pine, the beech, the zelkova, the Sargent juniper, and the *Carpinus laxiflora*. (I pay my respects to the bonsai enthusiasts of California who have transformed the desert Californian junipers into such fine specimens of bonsai that they surpass the Japanese *Itoigawa* junipers.)

BONSAI STYLES

Bonsai are modeled after their natural shape, so it is best to train a bonsai to form a specific style in keeping with the natural form of the species. This is done by a) removing buds, b) pruning branches, c) changing the curve of the trunk and branches through the process of wiring, and d) positioning the roots.

The following styles, shown on pages 13–20, are the most common bonsai patterns used in Japan, but just as a bonsai reflects the culture and personality of its owner, so bonsai in America, which is still in its infant stages, may grow to reflect the culture of the country as well as the personality of its owner.

Straight Trunk

The trunk in this type of bonsai is straight with branches growing just above the roots and tapering to a point. The roots should be distributed equally around the tree. The branches should grow from all around the trunk and should be well spaced. The Japanese cypress, the Japanese cedar, the juniper, the Japanese larch, the five-needle pine, and the Japanese black pine are ideal examples of straight trunk trees.

Slanting Trunk

This style of bonsai is cultivated at a slant, imitating trees found along windswept beaches or on mountaintops. Due to the windy conditions, the branches grow more heavily on one side of the trunk than the other and in some cases one side of the trunk may be completely bare. Junipers and pines are trained in this style.

Twin Trunk

This style has two trunks growing from a single root. If both trunks are of roughly the same size it is called a twin-trunk bonsai, but if one is bigger than the other, then it is called a parent and child bonsai. Pines, junipers, and most deciduous species can be grown in this style.

Triple Trunk

This style of bonsai may have three, five, or seven trunks growing from a single root. It is also possible to have more than seven trunks, which is another style of bonsai. Slender-trunked trees like maples are best suited to this style, for the many trunks make the bonsai resemble a grove.

Sinuous Root

This style resembles the group bonsai below, but the trunks grow from a single root, which sprout smaller roots and thus gives the bonsai the appearance of separate trees. Pines and junipers (*communis* L.), and some wild trees have this characteristic.

Raft

This style is effected by placing the trunk horizontally in the soil and arranging the branches vertically so they will grow like trunks.

Group

This bonsai is fundamentally a group of trees planted and arranged to resemble a small forest. Most people like this style because it reminds them of a walk in the woods. Trees should not be of the same height or the same shape since this is not the way they grow in nature. Of all the different styles of bonsai this group cultivation is the easiest to achieve. You can grow any number you like and combine any trees together, but it is best not to use trees with large fruit for this style.

Twisted Trunk

This bonsai, as its name suggests, has a twisted trunk and crooked branches. It is a mystery how trees like this survive in their natural environment of strong winds and rain, or why the piece of trunk that withers turns ashen white like a piece of bone. This phenomenon, known as *jin,* cannot be cultivated. The wild juniper and the *Juniperus communis* are perfect for the twisted trunk style.

Cascading

This kind of tree is found on mountains and the bonsai counterpart should be cultivated to suggest mysterious and wild regions, such as canyons. The root should be one-sided. Pines and junipers are ideal for this shape, although a semi-cascading style in which the branches do not droop so low is suitable for all species of trees.

Patterned

The trunk and branches of this bonsai are specially cut and shaped to give a curved appearance. The most elegant of all these patterned shapes is called *bunjin* (literati) bonsai. The Japanese red pine, the Japanese black pine, the spruce and the maple are by far the best kinds of trees for this style of bonsai.

Rock-grown

This style of bonsai is grown on stone. The tree can either be planted in the cavities of a rock or stone buried in soil, or it can be grown on exposed rock and the roots covered with sand. In the first style, place the bonsai in a deeper pot, and in the second, use a shallow tray, which can be filled with pebbles and water.

As I mentioned earlier, bonsai will gradually acclimatize to any environment through the process of cultivation. It is, therefore, worth repeating the three key factors that contribute to the correct growth and development of bonsai.

Just as man cannot live without water, air, and sunlight, so your bonsai have to be carefully nourished by these three elements in order to survive. Watering is the first important step to bear in mind.

Bonsai are grown in very small pots containing a limited amount of soil and, therefore, must be watered constantly and regularly to prevent them from withering. In watering your bonsai, it is best to use a sprinkling can since this wets the foliage and prevents the topsoil from being washed away.

There is no hard and fast rule concerning the frequency of watering your bonsai—it all depends on the species. Some trees, like maple, cedar, and cypress, need more water than others, but in general when the topsoil becomes a little dry (not too dry), it is time to water your tree. Water only until there is a leakage from the drainage hole. Too much water will rot the roots or will encourage the leaves and branches of the tree to grow too quickly.

The roots of a bushy tree are more numerous and tend to get dry more quickly. So frequent checks for dryness should be made every day. You must not forget to water the tree in the evening by sprinkling from above to wet the foliage.

Foliage sprinkling not only removes dust from leaves and branches, but also restores the shape of the bonsai after repotting, as well as helping buds to grow after pruning. Be careful when sprinkling the foliage during the day. A drop of water on a leaf has the same burning effect as the lens of a magnifying glass.

The best water for bonsai is, of course, rainwater, which contains minerals and natural nutrients. It is a good idea to save rainwater in a container, especially in areas like Southern California where rainwater is scarce during many months of the year.

Another good water source is well water. During the summer well water should be kept in a jug to warm up a little before using it on bonsai. In winter the water can be pumped up and used directly.

For those who live in the city there is a special nozzle sold today which can be attached to the hose and will purify tap water. This is a desirable way of eliminating polluting elements in tap water.

The second key point to remember is air. Your bonsai breathes through its roots as well as through its foliage, so the selection of soil mixture as well as the grade of soil is very important. Repotting is one good source of air, but I will discuss this in more detail in Chapter 3.

The last point I want to mention is sunlight. Contrary to accepted belief, sunlight is not always necessary for bonsai. Some trees flourish in strong sun, others in early morning sun, and still others don't need strong sunlight at all. It helps to see the tree in its natural setting before determining how much sunlight it needs when it is cultivated as bonsai.

Trees and Shrubs Used for Bonsai

American East Coast Maple

Collected American Crab Apple
North American Alberta Spruce

Pitch Pine (and detail)

American East Coast
Tamarack (and detail)

Blaauw's Juniper

Montezuma Cypress

Black Spruce

American Hazelnut

Norwegian Spruce

Swiss Mountain Pine
(and detail)

Californian Juniper   Hollywood Juniper   Golden Cup Oak

Pomegranate   Prostrata Juniper

Silver-Blue Atlas Cedar   Silver-Blue Atlas Cedar

Elm

Japanese Maple

Pyracantha

Hawaiian Pine
(and detail)

Black Pine

Ohia Lehua of Hawaii

Bougainvillea

BONSAI STYLES

A Straight Trunk Bonsai

A Slanting Trunk Bonsai

A Multiple Trunk Bonsai

A Twin Trunk Bonsai

A Triple Trunk Bonsai

A Sinuous Root Bonsai

Group Bonsai

Group Bonsai

A Cascading Bonsai

A Semi-cascading Bonsai

A Twisted Trunk Bonsai

A Patterned Bonsai

34

A "Literati" Patterned Bonsai

A Rock-grown Bonsai

Bonsai planted in rock cavities

Bonsai planted on exposed rock

Moss

Bryum argenteum L.

Weisia viridula Hedw.
Pogonatum contortum Lesq.
"Silver" Fungi

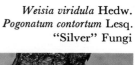

Unglazed china; medium-deep; blue-gray and brick red.

Unglazed china; shallow; blue-gray.

Decorated unglazed china; medium-deep; brown.

Unglazed china; shallow; white and blue.

Glazed china; medium-deep; blue.

Earthenware pots.

Decorated pots.

Pots for miniature bonsai.

Bonsai are cultivated in small pots. The soil, therefore, is essential since it provides moisture for the roots. As a general rule, bonsai grow best in the soil of their natural habitat. For example, Californian junipers thrive in slightly alkaline soil, while other species (with the exception of azaleas) need soil containing about PH_4 acidity. But in most cases bonsai are not cultivated in their natural environment and thus the soil type should be selected with care. Generally speaking, a combination soil is preferable to a basic soil, and in most cases, a sandy soil, either river or granite sand, is mixed with basic soil because sand retains water well. (Of these, river sand collected from upstream is better because the grains consist of squarish particles that do not pack the soil too densely.) But any type of soil can be used, including volcanic soil, as long as it a) retains moisture, b) allows ventilation, and c) has a neutral reaction.

Sandy soil allows roots to breathe and retains moisture to prevent roots from withering. The roots are also stimulated by the coarse soil particles resulting in better root differentiation. Fine soil or heavy clay soil should never be used since they do not meet any of the above three requirements. Recently it has been found that volcanic soil is good for bonsai because each grain has a bubble of air in it which acts like a dam. For sandy soil, it is best to sift it first through a sieve to remove any foreign objects. The University of California has researched soil for potting plants and this potting soil can be bought in bulk from nurseries in America.

I mention the third point especially for those who are experimenting with new species, since the best type of basic soil to use is one with a *neutra reaction*. You can then make it more acidic by adding redwood sawdust or peat moss, or more alkaline by mixing it with limestone sand. Never use ocean sand because of the harmful salt content in it. With all these soils, check to see if they are free of fungus before buying.

Potting soil from
the University of California

Redwood sawdust

Moss

Moss is always grown with bonsai for two good reasons. Not only does moss blend well together with bonsai but it also retains water and holds the soil together, thus preventing it from spilling over when you water the tree.

Moss can grow quite naturally in a pot since spores from the moss fall off during watering and will grow from the soil. But if you want better moss in your pot, you can cultivate it from these three species: a) *Bryum argenteum* L., a long and silvery species; b) *Weisia viridula* Hedw., thick and green, like brocade; and c) *Pogonatum contortum* Lesq., which resembles a small forest.

These are the most common species of moss used in Japan, although other species can also be planted with bonsai. Those to be avoided, however, are the liverwort, the *Dumortiera hirsuta* Nees, the *Marchantia polymorpha* L., and the *Pellia Neesiana* Raddi. These species of moss tend to form in pots that are too wet, and if they appear they should be weeded out immediately.

How to Transfer Moss into a Pot

1. With a small trowel or shovel (*1*), scoop up the moss taking care not to remove too much soil with it. Place the moss on a sheet of paper in a box (*2*), and water it with a sprinkling can or nozzle until the moss is moist.

2. Prod the surface soil with the tips of a pair of tweezers, and sweep about 3/16 in. of the new surface with a hand broom (*3, 4*).

3. Remove as much of the soil from the moss as is possible with a pair of scissors (*5*).

4. Separate the moss into small portions (big ones may not take root), and remove any foreign substance from it (*6*).

5. Spread some fine soil over the exposed surface in the pot (7).

6. Place the first pieces of moss a little away from the base of the trunk and continue placing the moss toward the tips of the branches (8). Do not plant moss closely around the base of the trunk since this prevents sunshine from getting to the roots and the roots will not thicken. Scatter soil over the moss until only the tips are visible (9).

7. Press the soil down with a trowel or the spatulate part of a pair of tweezers (10).

8. Water with a sprinkling can or a nozzle (11). Ten minutes later water once again. The soil scattered over the moss will settle among the moss quite naturally. Always remember that moss should be kept moist before it is planted in the pot. In two weeks or so the moss will start sprouting from the soil surface.

How to Sow Moss

This is a very simple procedure which even a beginner can tackle efficiently. Sowing moss is also useful if you are potting a great number of trees or when moss is in short supply. Today a number of nurseries sell moss but it is more interesting to sow your own.

1. Transfer moss (*see* above) with a trowel or shovel and keep it in the shade for two days to dry.

2. After it is dry, screen it through a sieve (1/24 in. mesh) and crumble it into fine particles (*12*).

3. Mix this with two or three times the amount of soil (*13*).

4. Spread this thinly over the surface soil in the pot, without removing any of it beforehand (*14*).

5. Press the soil down with a trowel or the spatulate part of a pair of tweezers (*15*).

6. Water with a fumigator, not a sprinkling can, to prevent the dry moss from flowing away with the water. Continue using the fumigator for a week or until the moss turns slightly greenish. (This method takes one week longer than the former in order for the moss to turn green.)

When your bonsai is thriving, a beautiful, silvery fungus will form on the trunk close to the soil. This is a fungus, not a moss, belonging to the group of bacteria called bryophyta. This fungus, generally mistaken for moss, always grows on a good bonsai and is one way of showing the age of the tree. Regretfully, this fungus cannot be attached to the tree artificially, so you must wait for it to grow naturally. It is also a good barometer for telling whether or not the moss cultivation is adequate. It appears most frequently when the soil in the pot is rather dry and sunlight penetrates to the roots of the tree.

Bonsai Diseases

Like ordinary trees, bonsai are also susceptible to disease and insects. When you make your daily rounds, check that the color of the leaves is healthy, and there are no insect droppings on the shelves. Prevent diseases by spraying the leaves with insecticides once in a while. These can be purchased from all nurseries. Dilute the insecticide with water according to the label directions and make sure that you spray the underneath part of the leaves until the insecticide falls into the soil.

Bonsai Pots

Chinese pots are best for bonsai because they have all the necessary conditions—good ventilation, good drainage, heat induction—for healthy growth. They are also appreciated as artistic objects. But they are scarce today, and Japanese pots produced in the Tokoname area near Nagoya, are good substitutes. They are also inexpensive, readily available, and come in all shapes and sizes. Some examples of bonsai pots are shown on page 36.

Pots are selected to suit the shape of the tree, and the 2,000 different kinds of pots can be classified according to the three following features: a) the material the pot is made from; b) the shape of the pot; c) its suitability to bonsai. Taking the first point, the material of the pot, they can be further subdivided into porcelain pots, china pots, and earthenware pots.

Porcelain Pots

The pot made from porcelain has a white base over which a colored glaze is applied, with birds, flowers or landscapes painted on the glaze. These pots come from the Seto district in Japan and are tall and deep, either round or hexagonal in shape. Large basins for bonsai are also being made in Seto today. Most porcelain pots are glazed, with the exception of some partially glazed porcelain pots that are also available.

China Pots

These are produced in the Tokoname district. They are part-white and part-colored and can be subcategorized into glazed and unglazed pots.

Of the unglazed variety there are seven distinct types depending on the color. The pots can be brown, brick red, greenish, yellow, purple, black, or sandy-colored. In the making of all these pots sand is first mixed with the clay.

The glazed variety of pots can also be divided into four categories. There is a blue or red glaze with tiny white dots on it, a bright blue glaze, a celadon glaze, and an ash-blue glaze modeled on Chinese pots.

Earthenware Pots

These pots have very rough surfaces and are today used for bonsai. They come either glazed or unglazed but only the bigger pots are made in earthenware.

Selecting your Pot

Bonsai pots should be selected with care according to the species and shape of the trees planted in them. Special attention should be paid to the shape, color, and size of the pot.

(A) SHAPE

The shape of the pot is of fundamental importance in the art of bonsai, and different species should be planted in different pots. For pines and other coniferous trees with straight trunks, a square or oblong pot that is not too deep is best. For most deciduous trees, use a shallow, rectangular or oblong pot. The patterned bonsai and the slanting style of bonsai are also best suited to these oblong, medium-deep pots.

Trees planted in a group are suited to rectangular or oblong, shallow pots that give a feeling of breadth. In a mixed species group planting use a medium-deep pot instead of a shallow pot.

In the cascading style of bonsai, a deep, round or square pot is best, while for a half-cascading bonsai, a deep, square pot is most appropriate.

(B) COLOR

The color of the pot is as important as its shape if you want your bonsai to look its best. Here are a few general principles to follow when choosing the color of the pot.

Pines and other coniferous trees are best suited to quiet colors, e.g. brown, purple or brick red. Most deciduous species should be planted in glazed celadon green pots or glazed blue pots speckled with white dots.

With flowering and fruit trees, choose a pot with a contrasting color that emphasizes the color of the flower or fruit, so do not put a tree with red flowers in a red pot, or a tree with white flowers in a white pot.

(c) SIZE

After you have selected the shape and color of the pot the next point to consider is the size. With the exception of the patterned trees and the group plantings, there is a simple rule of thumb that is easy to remember. The width of the pot should be two-thirds the height of the tree or the spread of its lowest branches (depending on which is used as the method of selection). For instance, if the tree is 15 inches tall, the pot should be 10 inches wide; and if the spread of the longest branches measures 18 inches, the pot should be 12 inches wide. (For comparison, the maple tree used in "Repotting" on page 65 is 25 inches tall. Its branch spread is 24 inches from left to right and 25 inches from front to back. The pot is 18 inches wide.)

Planting Position in the Pot

Finding the best position for the bonsai will show the tree to its greatest effect. *Never* plant the bonsai squarely in the middle of the pot. The best position is obtained by bearing in mind a certain ratio between the pot and the tree, such as 1:1.5 or 1:2 or 2:3 or 3:5 or 5:7. The most famous bonsai always keep the "magic" proportion of 7:12 or 38:62—applied to the ratio between the height of the tree and the spread of its branches, between the height of the tree and the position of its branches, and between the size of its trunk and the tapering of its branches.

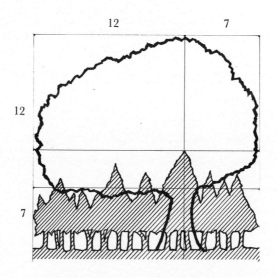

CHAPTER 2

GROWING BONSAI

There are many ways of cultivating bonsai. They can be grown from seeds, from seedlings collected in hills or fields, from cuttings, from graftings, from layering, from wild trees, or from bonsai bought at nurseries.

Growing Bonsai from Seeds

Numerous varieties of seeds can be bought from bonsai nurseries or even florists in the United States. Recently, seeds of Japanese trees are being stocked in these stores, such as the five-needle pine, the Japanese black pine, the Japanese hornbeam, the Japanese beech, the Japanese zelkova, the Japanese maple, and the wax tree. Just follow the directions on the back of the seed pack.

Growing Bonsai from Natural Seedlings

A one- or two-year-old tree collected from hills or fields for its shape and degree of health may be potted and trained as bonsai. I will give you a few rules to follow when potting your "natural" bonsai.

1. The best time to do this is just as winter is ending and when the tree is waking up and its roots are becoming active. With the exception of mid-summer, the tree will grow at all times provided you treat it with great care.

2. If the tree is one year old, you can use either a quarter-gallon can or a six-inch shaping pot. If you use the can, cut off one-third of the top of the can since you won't need such deep soil (unless you want the bonsai to grow from a stone, in which case you want deep soil to encourage longer roots). If you plan to use the can for shaping the tree, you will need some stainless steel or vinyl mesh to plug the drainage hole. This will keep the soil from flowing away when you water it, and keep the water flowing well. It will also keep insects out.

3. To screen the soil, you will need three sieves: a 1/16 in. mesh, a 1/8 in. mesh, and a 3/16 in. mesh sieve. First eliminate the fine soil with the 1/16 in. mesh, next put the soil through the 1/8 in. mesh, and the remainder through the 3/16 in. mesh. Line the bottom of the pot with the soil that did not go through the 3/16 in. mesh, and then fill half the pot with soil from the 3/16 in. mesh sieve.

4. To pot the tree, dig it out carefully, taking care not to damage the tiny roots just underneath the trunk (*1*).

5. Cut off the burdocklike root at right angles to the trunk (*2*). Use a sharp root cutter, not any blunt tool. The way the roots are cut will deter-

mine the distribution of roots as well as the trunk and branch structure of your bonsai in the future.

6. Distribute the roots evenly around the trunk, keeping them straight all the time (*3*). This is a new discovery in bonsai-growing. A tree with an uneven root distribution loses half its beauty. (I will explain on p. 95 how to correct roots that are unbalanced or have poor distribution.) If there are any roots protruding, cut them off but do not push them into the soil.

7. Cover the roots with soil from the 1/8 in. mesh sieve and push it down gently with a rake (*4*).

8. Fill 90 percent of the pot with soil, piling it higher around the base of the tree toward the middle of the pot (*5*).

9. Push this down with a trowel (*6*), and secure the tree to the pot by tying soft string around it and the pot (*7*).

10. Water the bonsai from the top with a sprinkling can or nozzle until the drainage hole begins to show seepage.

48

From Cuttings

The biggest advantage of cuttings is that you can visualize the result from the parent tree. The best time to take cuttings is just after the tree buds, although deciduous trees may be cut in fall as they tend to be very sticky after sprouting. New branches are best, although any branches can be used, even last year's or older.

Before you take the cutting, consider the shape you want the bonsai to form in the future. If you want a straight trunk bonsai, take the cutting together with the stem from the central branch or the top of the trunk. If you prefer a slanting trunk or cascading style, then you should take a branch cutting since branches grow at an angle.

You can use any soil that is free of bacteria and other impurities as long as it has good ventilation, good drainage, and retains water. You can choose a compost that blends river sand with garden soil, perlite, or a mixture of vermiculite with peat.

Always take the cuttings from the mother tree (*8*). A few cuttings are easily placed in a deep pot, and one or two cuttings are best planted together with the mother tree (*9*). In natural surroundings you can see that young trees always grow around the mother tree, so this method follows the same idea (*10*). If you are taking a lot of cuttings, it is best to arrange a special cuttings bed for them.

HOW TO TAKE A CUTTING OF ROCK COTONEASTER

In order to illustrate what I have said, I will show you how to take a cutting from this tree. I have selected the rock cotoneaster because its shape is ideal for bonsai, its leaves are small, and it buds easily. In addition, it flowers during spring and tiny clusters of fruit appear in the fall.

1. You will need a deep pot or a wooden box, a sieve, soil bucket, scissors, tweezers, watering can or nozzle, vinyl or stainless steel mesh, soil, wire, and a wash basin or bowl (*11*).

2. Place the vinyl mesh over the drainage hole of the pot and secure with wire (*12, 13*).

3. Spread large particles of soil as directed in the section on potting (*14*) (*see* p. 47). Arrange the soil so that it rises in the center and slopes away toward the rim of the pot.

4. Take the cutting, 2 to 4 inches long, from just under the bud at right angles to it (*15, 16*), since the part nearest the buds takes root easily. (The angle is important for the correct distribution of roots around the tree.) Before planting, cut off the leaves that will be buried underground. Another point to remember is to use sharp scissors when taking the cutting since blunt ones can damage the branch or spoil its shape.

5. Soak the cutting in water for thirty minutes as soon as it is cut (*17*).

6. Make a few holes in the soil an inch or two apart. Pick up the cutting with tweezers and plant the main branch into the soil at a slant (*18–20*). For the best chance of success, pick up the cutting with the tips of the tweezers over the cut end so as not to damage it (*21*).

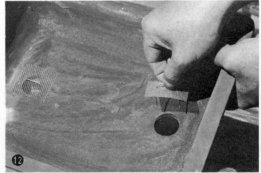

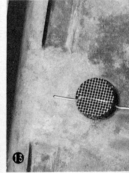

7. Water well, from the top (*22*).

8. The rock cotoneaster grows easily, so it is good to place the pot in a light, sunny position. Roots will begin to grow after one month. When the roots are about two inches long, pot them in the same way as directed on pages 47 and 48.

9. Compare this tree two years after potting (*23*) with one that was shaped eight years ago (*24*). In any cutting you can select the style you want—a single branch will turn into a bonsai with a single trunk, two branches into twin trunks, and three branches into triple trunks (*25, 26*). Cuttings can be taken from any species but the most popular are: Californian juniper, *Ezo* spruce, Japanese cypress, Japanese cedar, azalea, pomegranate, weeping willow, camellia, Japanese maple, Japanese zelkova, and rock cotoneaster.

51

From Graftings

Bonsai that have been grafted grow more quickly than those planted from seedlings but I personally do not consider them good bonsai. Even though they have been well grafted, it is impossible to hide the bumps, and with the exception of some special trees, they have little or no value.

In Japan grafting is used most frequently for flowering and fruit trees, or to increase the seeds of five-needle pines, or to make small clusters. There are two types of grafts: branch grafts, when you want to add a branch where the tree is bare, and spliced grafts, used for young trees.

(A) BRANCH GRAFT

1. The best time for grafting is just before budding. Cut into the trunk of a large branch with a flat chisel until the chisel touches the xylem (*1, 2*). Make sure that the incision is made where the branch is relatively straight and smooth for this will facilitate taking.

2. Cut off a one-year-old slip from the mother tree (*3*) and shape the end into a wedge (*4, 5*).

3. Insert the wedged end into the trunk (6) and bind them together with vinyl tape, not too tightly (7).

4. Cover this over with a polythene bag to preserve moisture and to assure the best chances of success (8). (It is also a good idea to make two grafts and if both of them take then cut one off.) You can make as many grafts as you like onto the tree at the same time, as shown on the wistaria (9).

(B) SPLICED GRAFT

Place two pots side by side (*1*). Cut into the xylems of both trunks and bind the two trunks together with vinyl tape (*2*). When the two trunks are growing well together, cut the trunks just underneath the graft (*3*). This method is used for species which are difficult to graft with branch grafts.

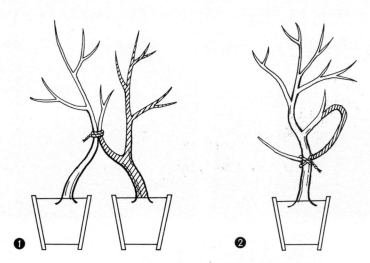

Layering

This method is a faster way of growing a new bonsai than from cuttings. Furthermore, you can use anything from a good branch in your garden to a discarded branch from your old bonsai. Layering is also a good way of improving root distribution. The best time to do this is during the rainy season, or in regions where there is little rain, when the new buds have sprouted and the leaves are fully grown. Not all species will take root easily, but among the best types of trees to use in layering are the five-needle pine tree, the Japanese black pine, the *Ezo* spruce, the Japanese cedar, the juniper, the Japanese maple, the Japanese zelkova, and the pomegranate.

(A) LAYERING BY WIRING

This is one of two ways of layering used for bonsai and is most suitable for trees of the pine family.

1. Tightly bind the trunk selected for layering with wire and cut off the surplus ends of wire (*1–3*).

2. Prepare enough sphagnum moss to go around the trunk three or four times. Wrap moss around the wired trunk, cover this with a polythene bag, and bind with vinyl tape (*4, 5*).

3. Make one opening at the top and one at the bottom of the bag to ensure that water flows well, watering enough so the moss does not dry out.

4. A month or two later new buds will appear, and roots will grow underneath the wired area. This means that the sap has stimulated the growth of new roots.

5. When new roots start to touch the wrapping, the tree should be repotted. When you take the moss off, take care that you do not damage the new roots (6). Cut the tree as close to the new roots as possible, at right angles to the trunk. Repot only after you have pruned all surplus branches so that they do not use the moisture intended for the roots. (*See* "Repotting.")

(B) LAYERING BY CUTTING OFF THE BARK

This method is ideal for bonsai which have been potted in a shallow pot and then repotted in a deeper one.

1. Make two horizontal cuts, at a distance of twice the thickness of the trunk (7).

2. Shave off the bark and cambium and continue to cut into the trunk toward the xylem (8, 9). If you do not cut deep enough, the old root will continue to be nourished and the shaved section will not sprout new roots. New roots will not grow where the cambium has been left on the trunk.

3. Wrap and bind with moss as directed in the section above. (If you use this as a method for improving root distribution, shave off the bark and cover the shaved area with soil instead of wrapping with vinyl tape.) Be careful not to let the base of the trunk get dry.

From Wild Trees

Wild trees, according to species and shape, can also be cultivated as bonsai. The type of tree which adapts most easily to cultivation in a pot is the tree with small branches and leaves, or with fine roots that thrive in a small pot.

Among the species naturally suited for bonsai in America are the Californian juniper, the most representative bonsai of America, the cherrystone juniper (*Juniperus monosperma*) of the Arizona desert, and the Utah juniper (*Juniperus osteosperma*) from the Utah valleys. The last two species are not commonly used by bonsai enthusiasts in America, and I should like to encourage their usage.

From the pine family there is the American pitch pine (*Pinus rigida* Mill), with short leaves resembling the Japanese black pine. There is also the shore pine (*Pinus contorta*), the lodgepole pine (*Pinus murrayana*), and the Mugo pine (*Pinus mugo pumilio*).

A few other trees like the Canadian hemlock (*Tsuga canadensis*), the canyon oak (*Quercus chrysolepis lobman*)—both of which have small leaves—the Chinese elm (*Ulmus parvifolia*), the beech (*Fagus grandifolia*), and the mountain laurel (*Kalmia latifolia*) are also good for bonsai.

The mountain laurel, the state flower of Connecticut, is found all over the United States from New Brunswick to Texas to Ohio. The tree belongs to the rhododendron family and prefers an acidic soil, a point to remember when mixing your soil.

These are a few of the wild species suited to bonsai cultivation, but it is up to you to experiment with others. Do not repot these bonsai for two years, but concentrate more on root distribution.

From Bonsai Bought at Nurseries

Bonsai sold in nurseries are either gathered from mountains and trained, or grown from seeds. When buying a tree you should watch out for a few points, which I shall list below.

1. Look for trees where the branches are well balanced and well spaced, a sign that the distribution of roots is even.

2. Check to see if the leaves are shining and healthy, another sign of healthy roots. A good growth of branches will also reflect the health and good distribution of the roots. If a tree has a lot of branches, the excess branches can be cut off, starting low from the trunk.

3. The trunk of a good bonsai should taper toward the tip. Avoid those with thick, stumpy tips, which show that they have been cut off from the top, a sign that the tree is growing too fast and may not be ideal for bonsai.

4. Look out for cracks and scars on the trunk. Although pines and junipers have natural scars and cracks on the trunks, avoid other species when they have scratched trunks, especially maples and zelkovas. But do not mistake the shaped stem which has cracks of a tree collected from the wilderness for a scarred trunk.

5. Do not select bonsai whose branches show an unnatural bend, a sign of overwiring during shaping. Bonsai enthusiasts prefer a tree with a natural curve and this is apparent from its natural shape, which is then improved when it is wired and pruned.

6. Check for signs of disease or insects, since they may infect other trees. Most bonsai grown from seedlings have roots that have already been trimmed. With natural, wild bonsai, the roots are still untrimmed, so trim the roots first before you pot them. Then look after them in the same way as bonsai that have been grown from seedlings or from cuttings.

CHAPTER 3

REPOTTING

Bonsai are planted in small containers. As the roots grow they break up the soil and this prevents water from reaching every part of the roots. This is why they have to be repotted frequently: otherwise stunted branches and rotted roots will result. Since not all trees develop at the same rate, it is difficult to pinpoint the exact frequency of repotting. Some have to be repotted once a year, others can survive five to seven years in the same pot, but the trained bonsai enthusiast can tell at a glance if a tree needs repotting. Two simple guidelines are listed below.

1. The soil level in the pot should usually be just below the edge to prevent soil from escaping during watering and to allow water to reach every part of the pot. When the soil rises over the rim of the pot, it is a sign that the roots have spread out too far, pushing the soil upward. This tells you it is time for repotting.

2. When roots grow through the drainage hole at the bottom of the pot, repotting is absolutely necessary. Repotting can also serve to correct a disproportional root growth but I will discuss this in more detail on page 95.

The best time to repot a bonsai is in the spring, when buds appear on the branches. This is when the tree is at its "strongest"—when the roots are stimulated by sunlight and are becoming active. In winter the roots are definitely not active enough to withstand repotting.

One exception, however, is the five-needle pine, which should be repotted when the leaves are coming out. Another is the flowering quince (*Chaenomeles sinensis*), which, because it is easily afflicted by threadworm, should be repotted in the fall. (I have heard, but not tested, the theory that marigolds planted close by will rid the tree of threadworm.) You should treat your bonsai more carefully when you repot in the fall, because the tree is more fragile then than in the spring.

Repotting a Japanese Maple

At first glance this maple looks as if its trunks are all connected, but in actual fact it was grown from many seedlings and first potted fifteen years ago. It resembles a wild maple, but the thinness and elegance of its branches betray its real species.

1. I last repotted this tree two years ago and since then the soil has risen above the edge of the pot (*1*): time for repotting. The present pot is too large for the tree and I plan to use a smaller oval pot. As I said earlier, the

pot is an integral part of bonsai, like clothes, so to speak, and so a pot which is most suited to the bonsai should be used.

2. Cut around the edge of the pot with a sickle (*2*). Since roots grow all over the pot, it is essential not to damage them. Using a turntable is a great help since it is easy to cut around the pot while turning it.

3. When the tree is lifted out of the pot (*3*) the thin rootlets that have grown around the edge of the pot and into the drainage hole will have to be disentangled. Do this from the outside and work inward with a rake (*4*).

4. Remove two-thirds of the soil clinging to the roots and smooth the roots into the shape of a star.

5. Disentangle the roots just under the trunk (*5*).

6. Notice how long the roots have become (*6*). Trim the longer ones with a sharp pair of scissors, cutting them off at the place where they hang downward (*7*). The correct length is about 1 to $1\frac{1}{2}$ in. below the new soil level.

7. Roots just underneath the trunk are cut at right angles to the trunk, just under the area where the soil is still clinging to the roots (*8*).

8. The remaining roots should be trimmed. Take special care not to use blunt scissors, since this will cause the roots to rot. Now compare the trimmed roots (*9*) with (*3*).

9. Prepare the new pot (*10*). You will need stainless steel or vinyl mesh and aluminum or vinyl wires with diameters of 1/16 and 1/32 in. (Iron and steel mesh and wires should never be used because they rust and damage the roots.)

10. The wires are cut into appropriate lengths to tie the mesh over the drainage hole and to tie the roots later. To do this, the wire is inserted into the hole from the outside, through the mesh (*11–14*).

11. Spread a layer of gravel soil (*15*) and a layer of potting soil (*16*) over it in the pot. Heap it slightly at the place where the trunk is to be planted. The mound prevents empty spaces from forming. Notice that the trunk is not placed in the center of the pot (*17*).

12. When the position of the tree is selected, tie the roots carefully (*18*). They should not be too tight. There should be enough room to insert a finger inside the wire, which will allow room for expansion. Cut off the surplus wire.

13. The soil is placed in the pot (*19*). Use more than is necessary, and

prod it with a rake in order to fill the empty spaces in between the roots (20). Take care not to damage any of the roots. Press down the soil with your fingertips, making sure the soil is packed tightly around the roots (21) to help them grow. The excess soil is brushed away with a hand broom (22).

14. Press the surface soil with a trowel (23), using a firmer pressure for evergreens than for deciduous trees. It is said that in the case of five-needle pines, the soil should be pounded with a mallet, but I think experience is the only way to tell how much pressure should be applied. The soil level should be lower than the edge of the pot (24).

15. Place the pot on the turntable to check if the bonsai is planted in the right position (25), since it is impossible to repot once the tree is watered. Water the tree until there is a definite leak from the drainage hole. Then place the bonsai outdoors in the sun, unless there is a strong wind which could loosen the newly planted roots.

16. After this, watering must be done carefully (26). Now that the roots have been trimmed, their rate of absorption is lessened. Do not water the bonsai until the topsoil is dry. If the soil surrounding the roots is too wet, the roots will start to rot. Do *not* use fertilizers until at least two weeks later. Sunlight is especially good after repotting since it stimulates growth and dries the topsoil.

17. This is the repotted maple one month later (27). It was fertilized two weeks after repotting. If the leaves look healthy, it is a sign that the roots have taken hold.

18. The next two to three weeks are busy ones. Since the new leaves are growing well, they should be trimmed daily, to prevent them from growing too long and thick. For three weeks, the time required for the new leaves to mature, daily trimming is a necessary but pleasant chore. When trimming, do *not* remove the first pair of leaves, but trim off any irregular buds (28, 29).

19. After two months the new leaves will not grow so quickly and will turn a bright, vivid green. This is a sign that the leaves have become "stabilized" and a sign that they have to be trimmed by a different process. Generally speaking, this process of leaf-trimming is only reserved for the trident maple, the zelkova, and the Japanese maple, in order to keep the leaves small, the tops of the branches thin, and for the leaves to turn red in the fall. This procedure should only be performed on trees that are healthy and strong, about two-and-a-half months after repotting.

20. Cut the leaf stems with a special pair of scissors. Begin from the top of the tree because the leaf stems are easily visible from this angle (*30*). With the two species of maple cut from the center of the leaf stem, and with the zelkova cut at the base of the leaf.

21. Cut the leaves from the center of the leaf stem (*31*). Despite my care I find that some of the leaves have rotted and they must be cut off cleanly from the base with special nippers (*32–34*).

22. During the cutting I often find I have left some unwanted, irregular buds on the tree, and they must be cut off, as well as the thin, long branches (*35, 36*).

23. If you discover other long branches, or dead branches, cut these off from the base (*37*). Then place the bonsai in the sun and sprinkle water on the places that have been cut. Until new leaves appear, avoid watering the soil until it is completely dry. Water the leaves sparingly, since the soil will dry very slowly because of the reduced number of the leaves. In two weeks the leaves will reappear as before. Do not water the leaves during the day because of the hot sun, and place the bonsai in a spot where it will not be subject to the strong afternoon sun. This will make the leaves grow more beautifully, especially in the fall. Use fertilizers *only* in early fall—not in midsummer.

In this example the tree I used was a mature one and thus did not need wiring, but with the Japanese maple the best time for wiring is when the leaves are "hard." When the shape of the tree is not fully developed, wiring will produce the desired form. If you are wiring the bonsai after cutting, and if the tree is young and its bark tender, first wrap paper around the wire to prevent the bark from being scratched.

I did not trim the branches here although the usual time for this is just after repotting. The small branches can be cut off with nippers, but for larger branches use a chisel or a sculptor's knife. This way the scars will heal quickly and will not become prominent. This procedure also governs the appearance of the bonsai in the future.

10

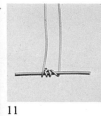

11

12

13

14

15

16

17

18

19

66

20

21

22

23

24

26

25

27

28   29

30   31

32   33   34

35   36   37

Repotting Other Species

Except for pines, all other types of trees can be repotted in the same way. Pines are slightly unusual. They grow with a "white mold." Thus the best time to repot a pine is when the mold grows profusely, when the buds begin to open. This occurs about the time you are trimming the leaves of your maple. At the end of summer, when the buds are hard, there is a second opportunity for repotting.

The pine repotted during this time will have fine white mold spreading over the drainage hole after ten days, a sign that the tree has caught root. Even if the roots are damaged a little, the resin oozing from them will repair the damage.

When repotting, sift the old soil so that the white mold is broken into smaller particles and mix this with the new soil. Then repot. The pine should be repotted every three years, not five or six as some people believe.

The tree should be kept at a temperature that stimulates the white mold and dries the topsoil by evening, if the pine is watered in the morning. This will ensure new vitality.

CHAPTER 4

WIRING

Bonsai grown from seedlings, cuttings, or layering and dividing are easily shaped by nipping the buds or trimming the leaves. But trees collected from the wilderness have to be correctly formed and trained to give them the right shape. This is where wiring is so essential. It is also the only way of altering the tree's shape completely. In the first instance all you need do by wiring is correct the curve of the branches, without touching the trunk at all, while in the second instance a lot more work is required to alter the shape of the tree completely. Here is a list of tools you will need for wiring. (All the numbers given in the list below, and mentioned elsewhere in the book, refer to the bonsai tools manufactured by Masakuni Co. Ltd., of Japan.)

WIRE CUTTER #7, #8, #9, #108 are used to cut all gages of wire, but all these cutters, except for #9, can also cut wire that has been wound around the trunk or imbedded in the trunk.

NIPPERS #18 are used to cut very thick wire.

TWEEZERS #10 are used for thin wires that are wound around the tips of branches.

LEVERS #25, #26, #116 will bend trunks or branches too thick to be bent by hand.

A JACK is used to bend trunks and branches with diameters of two to three inches.

A TURNTABLE is absolutely necessary for the wiring operation, since it can be turned and stopped at any position.

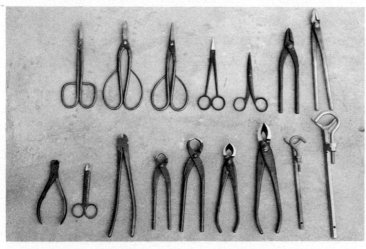

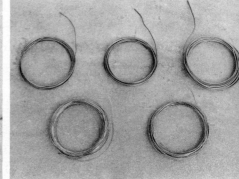

SHEARS #113, #114, #115 are used for splitting or cutting trunks in order to facilitate bending them.

TRIMMING SHEARS

Wiring is a process that acts in the same way as bandages, splints, and plaster casts. When one part of the branch or trunk is bent, that part is injured, so to speak, and the wires act like bandages that cannot be taken off until the broken area is healed. Annealed copper wires are best for this purpose because they are soft, pliable and do not rust, unlike steel wires. In addition, as time passes, the color of the copper wires will fuse with the trunk or branch and the wires will be invisible.

In recent years copper-colored aluminum wires have become available, but because they are softer than copper wires they cannot be used on larger branches or trunks, although they are excellent for wiring tips of branches or very small branches.

Wires come in different gages: #8, #10, #12, #14, #16, #18, #20 and #22. These are available from electrical appliance stores, hardware stores, or horticultural stores. Those sold in general hardware stores are not annealed, although I would recommend that you use annealed wire because it is easier to work with. Here is a simple way to anneal wire. Heat the wire up to a temperature of 842–932 degrees F. (You don't need a thermometer to calculate this because if wire is heated in a dark room, it begins to glow when the necessary temperature is reached.) You can either use your fireplace or barbecue grill for this purpose. Ten minutes heating is sufficient. Cool it in water if you are in a hurry. This annealed wire is ready for use.

The best time to wire for pines and other coniferous trees is in the winter, when the tree is hibernating. For flowering bonsai and deciduous trees it is best to wire when the buds have sprouted and the tree is growing quite rapidly.

It is better to wire in winter because the bark gets harder and will not damage easily. Even if the bark is damaged, resin will not flow too quickly from the damaged area and the tree will not weaken. There is one danger, however. The branches are more brittle and break easily, so just before wiring do not water the bonsai for one or two days, since without water, the trunk and branches become more pliant and will not break so readily.

When the tree is growing rapidly, the trunk and branches are soft, so even if they are damaged they will recover quickly. Always wire gently because the bark is soft and is easily damaged.

How to Wire a Five-Needle Pine

1. This tree is now ten years old and measures 12 in. (*1*). It has been repotted three times, but nothing more has been done to it, so its branches have grown in all directions. Place the bonsai on a turntable while you decided what shape to give it.

2. The lower trunk is very straight, then halfway from the ground it starts to bend a bit and straightens out at the top third of the trunk. It has numerous branches, so an upright style is best. (If a bonsai has very few branches then choose a patterned style instead.)

3. Once you have determined the style you can start trimming the surplus and unnecessary branches, like those which grow from one spot on the trunk in all directions (*2*). The branches should be cut off smoothly from the trunk with a knob cutter, either #35 or #36, and shears #16, #116, and #316 should be used for larger branches to make the cut concave in relation to the trunk (*3*). Start with the lowest branches first, then begin from the top. Make sure that the remaining branches are growing in a spiral and all receive enough sunshine and air. Cut off branches that are too weak or too strong, and trim off the tips of long branches that are not in proportion to the tree. Remember also that the branches should not be completely symmetrical on either side of the trunk. It is not necessary to keep the lowermost branches on the tree, but in order to encourage the trunk to thicken quickly, it is better to keep these branches as long as the trunk is too thin. (Be careful when you decide to cut these branches off. Once they are cut they will not grow again, except on the Mugo pine.)

4. After all the unnecessary branches have been cut off (*4*), you can proceed with wiring. Always wire the trunk first, followed by the lowermost branches and their twigs, then the second lowermost branches and twigs, and so on.

5. Before you start to wire the trunk, bend, or straighten out, the area to be wired with your hand (*5*). Then cut the wire a quarter the thickness of the trunk and 1.3 times its length (*6*).

6. Push the wire into the roots with nippers—the larger the better— to fix it firmly (*7*). Start binding with wire from below, not too tightly, but

you will get the correct feel with repetition. The wire should be held at an angle of 45 degrees to the trunk (*8*). See also that the wire twirls firmly around the area to be bent or straightened. Hold this part of the trunk with your hand as you wind wire around it.

7. In this case the trunk is too thick to be bent by hand, so I used a lever to do this (*9*).

8. After wiring the trunk, I wired the lowest branch, winding it from the trunk toward the tip of the branch (*10*). As I reach the tip where my fingers cannot easily twist the wire, I used a pair of tweezers #10. This is how all wiring is performed (*11*).

Sometimes small problems can occur, such as two branches growing very closely together. This is overcome by using one length of wire, tying the middle around the trunk and using the two ends, one for each branch, to wire the branches.

After the wiring is done, check to see if all the branches face upward (*12*) since they will weaken if they face downward. This is essential if the bonsai is to recover rapidly. I use the word "recover" because I think wiring a bonsai is like treating a broken leg with plaster of paris. Then water the leaves.

It takes from two months to six months for the tree to take on a permanent shape, depending on the age of the tree. It is not a good idea to keep the

⑪

⑫

wires on for too long because they become imbedded into the trunk and branches and there will be visible scars when they are removed.

Do not forget to take the wires off before fall, because this is the time the bonsai starts to grow again. Remove the wires from the uppermost tips of branches with tweezers (*13*), and then, with cutters (#7, #8, #108) remove the wires from the other parts of the tree (*14*). Do not try to unwind the wire from the end, since this just wastes time and could do damage to the branches.

CHAPTER 5

FERTILIZERS

Since bonsai grow and develop from spring to summer, they must store up nourishment in the fall to prepare for the winter. This is why fertilizers are given—not because they help the growth of bonsai over a short period. In fact too much fertilizer will cause the fine roots to rot, and, therefore, no fertilizer at all is better than an excessive amount.

The fertilizer you select for your bonsai should suit the species of tree as well as the type of soil. Despite the many chemical fertilizers on the market today, the best kind is still rape cake, made from rape seeds after the oil has been pressed out. A good fertilizer should contain the three necessary ingredients—nitrogen, phosphorus, and potassium—in proportionate quantities. To ensure that the bonsai grows well, the fertilizer used should "burn" slowly, a very important feature in America since sandy soil is used most of the time.

Rape cake is ideal for American bonsai because of this. There are two ways of preparing it, one when the oil is extracted through the use of benzene and other chemicals, and the other when the oil is pressed out of the seed. This is by far the better method since no valuable nutrient is lost by chemical action. It is also advisable to mix 20 percent of bone meal in the rape cake so as to increase the quantity of phosphorus and potassium in the fertilizer for fruit and flowering bonsai.

You may simply sprinkle the topsoil with powdered rape cake but the more effective method is to roll up four balls the size of your thumb and place these in the four corners of the pot (1). When the bonsai is watered the lumps will slowly disintegrate and work into the soil. Use fertilizers only in proportion to the size of the pot—for a pot that is 10 inches in diameter, use two tablespoons of rape cake.

To make the rape cake balls put the powder in a bowl and knead with water (2, 3). Do not add too much water and knead thoroughly or else the rape cake will turn lumpy. When the texture becomes soft, like putty, make thumb-sized round balls and leave them to dry before putting them in the pot (4). If you have fruit or flowering bonsai, add 20 percent bone meal during the kneading.

Rape cake can also be applied in liquid form. Pour the rape powder into a large jar, adding about ten times as much water to it (5, 6). Place the jar in strong sun and allow the mixture to ferment for a month. Use only the liquid part of the contents for the fertilizer. This fermented water should again be diluted by adding water in the ratio 1:10. Water your bonsai twice a month with this, making sure that *all* the soil is wet, not only the surface, but do not use too much of it since it is wasted if it flows through the drainage hole. In the case of miniature bonsai this liquid fertilizer can be applied with a syringe.

Correct Application of Fertilizers

1. Apply the fertilizers in spring just after the buds have appeared, since this is a sign that the roots have become active.

2. In the case of evergreen trees, fertilizers should be applied twice a month.

3. For deciduous trees, apply fertilizers only when buds have sprouted.

4. For fruit and flowering bonsai, fertilizers should be given just before they bear fruit or bloom, and just after the flowers have withered.

5. Do not use fertilizers just after repotting or when a tree has just been potted. Wait two weeks until the tree has taken root.

6. Never use fertilizers in midsummer.

7. Do not use fertilizers in winter since the tree is hibernating and its roots will not absorb the nourishment.

8. Consider the condition of the bonsai before applying fertilizers. A strong tree should not be given fertilizers and neither should a weak tree.

9. It is a good idea to use a little more fertilizer at the end of fall to help the tree prepare for winter, thus producing better results the following spring. You have to water the bonsai carefully after adding round balls of fertilizer in the fall, because the soil is drier in fall than in spring and the fertilizer's effectiveness can be halved. In fall the soil tends to dry faster because the tree is storing up nourishment for winter. It feels less sunshine as winter approaches. By feeding your bonsai with fertilizers during this period, you will be helping it prepare for hibernation. Use more fertilizer than you did in spring.

10. Remember, when you use fertilizers, use them in conjunction with the best natural sources of nutrition—sun, water, and air.

CHAPTER 6

BONSAI TOOLS

It is most important that bonsai tools be used correctly. Just as nobody would fish for sardines with tuna fish hooks, or play golf with the wrong clubs, it is unthinkable for a bonsai enthusiast to use the wrong tools for trimming, cutting, pruning, or wiring.

I would like to present a list of the most necessary tools for bonsai cultivators, describing the purpose and the correct handling of each. I believe it is vital for cultivators to handle tools correctly from the start. As a useful guide, the photographs will show you how to hold the tools, and I will explain the merits of each in turn.

Sieves (1)

Sieves are used to separate soil particles before use, and the smallest particles should be discarded because they block drainage, air ventilation, and retain water. A $\frac{1}{4}$ in. sieve in used to sift the soil, and the particles that remain in the sieve are placed at the bottom of the pot. Then, depending on the size of the pot, either a 3/16 or a 1/8 in. sieve is used in the same way. The remaining soil particles are placed in the pot. Next a 1/16 in. sieve is used. The soil remaining in the sieve is the planting soil, while the soil screened through it is the dressing soil. This dressing soil is passed through a 1/24 in. screen, and what remains on the screen is used for the bonsai.

Sieve Scoops (2)

The sieve does not always discard the smaller particles of soil and these scoops are essential for eliminating the remaining particles. This is specially useful for potting miniature bonsai.

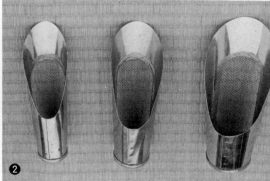

Gravers (3)
Their use is explained on pages 52, 56, 98.

Grafting Chisels (4, 5)
These tools are used for cutting into the xylem of the trunk as explained on pages 52, 56, 97, 98.

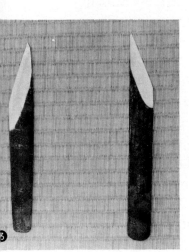
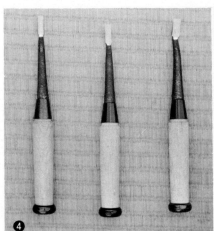
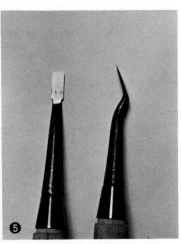

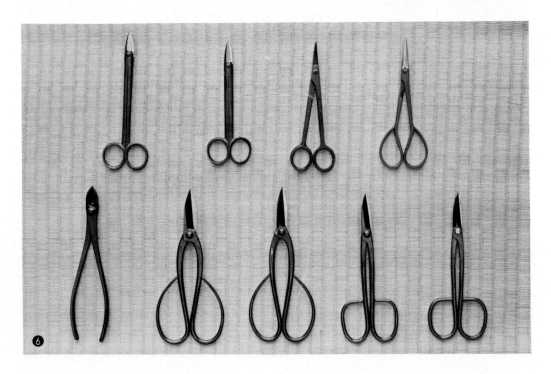

Bud-trimming Shears (*6*)

In general, trees have the tendency to grow upward rather than sideways. If the top branches of the bonsai are left alone, the lower branches will tend to wither, and if the buds are not trimmed from time to time, the branches will appear thick and unsightly. You have to take note of the position of the buds you leave on the tree so that branches and leaves will not criss-cross eventually. In most deciduous trees, buds are trimmed so that only the first two leaves are left on the branch (*7, 8*).

The shears used vary according to the hardness of the buds. For soft buds, use #3, #4, #5, #103. Shears #3 and #4 reach into the deep parts of the tree (*9*), and shears #5 and #103 are best for pines and junipers, although they are suitable for any other species as well (*10*). Their handles are spaced and, therefore, in trimming a pine, there is no danger of cutting off vital leaves and branches.

Shears #2, #28, #128, #216 are suited to hard buds (*11*). If you are trimming the base of the bud or new buds that grow in a fork, use shears #216 (*12*). These are good for cutting buds close to the base. The long blades make the cut invisible when the bud sprouts (*13, 14*). It is also effective for cutting off the tips of branches for shaping.

Leaf-trimming Shears (15)
These shears are used for trimming the leaves of the Japanese maple, the trident maple, and the zelkova. (*See* page 63 for their correct use.)

Branch-pruning Shears (16)
Branches are pruned when repotting or when planting the bonsai in a pot. For bonsai the branches should be as numerous as possible, with the lower ones longer than the upper ones. When the shape of the tree has already been formed, the buds must be trimmed regularly. If the shape has not been developed, the branches must be pruned so that the upper branches grow thinner and shorter than the ones underneath. After the bonsai has been pruned it should be left outdoors in the sun so as to encourage the lower branches to grow and develop.

Most beginners do not know where to start pruning the branches. I advise them to look at the natural shape of the tree and study its form. In a natural tree, or a good bonsai, all the branches grow in a natural pattern.

The lower branches spread out left and right, front and back, and they grow upward. Viewed from above, the branches resemble a spiral. This is the principle to follow when pruning a bonsai. (*see* sketch below).

Not all bonsai grow branches in this order. In some cases the branches will grow at longer intervals, and in others they will be so closely packed that the pruning operation becomes more difficult. I will explain this in detail later.

Here is a list of branches, called "loathsome" branches, that have to be cut off.

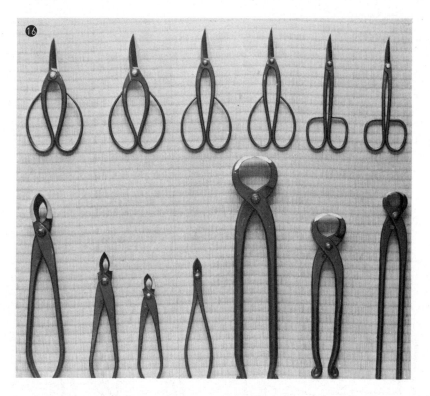
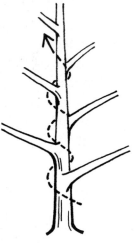

(A) ONE-SIDED BRANCHES

The best way to rectify this phenomenon is to change the style into a raft bonsai, where the trunk is buried horizontally, and the branches sprout like separate trees off a single root.

(B) PARALLEL BRANCHES

When two branches grow parallel on one side, cut one of them off.

(C) WHEEL BRANCHES

These branches usually grow on azaleas and pine trees. They sprout from one spot on the trunk in all directions. Cut the unnecessary branches off.

(D) UPRIGHT BRANCHES

Most of these upright branches are separate shoots and should be cut off whenever they appear. Otherwise, the section from the base of the new shoot to the tip of the old branch will weaken and wither.

(E) DROOPING BRANCHES

These downward-growing branches must be cut off. They interfere with the sunshine and ventilation of the other branches.

(F) CRISS-CROSSING BRANCHES

Branches that criss-cross spoil the shape of the tree and one of them has to be cut off, bent, or separated from the other.

(G) SYMMETRICAL BRANCHES

If two branches grow from one spot and fork to the left and right, one of them is usually cut off. In the case of an upright bonsai, cut off either of them. In the case of a curved bonsai, cut off the branch that is inside the curve.

(H) HORIZONTAL BRANCHES

Branches that cut straight across the trunk are unsightly and should be cut off.

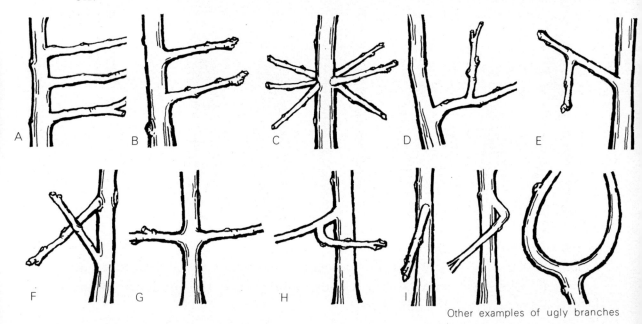

Other examples of ugly branches

92

(1) HOW TO CUT OFF FRONT BRANCHES

These branches are not considered desirable or beautiful in a bonsai and should be pruned. Use the large knob cutter #35 or the smaller one #36 to do this, or the shears #16, #116, #316, or #216. The knob cutter is used to cut off lumps formed on the tree trunk after the branches have been cut off (*1–10*). When these branches grow close together it is difficult to cut the middle one off with ordinary shears, so these four special ones are used (*11–14*). (They cut with a carving motion and do not cut straight across. They also leave a concave depression.)

When pruning smaller branches from midway up the trunk, shears #216 are best because the blades cut at a special angle. They are particularly effective for Sargent junipers, needle junipers, and spruces.

Shears #1 and #101 are used to prune branches the thickness of a pencil. To do this, press the branch downward with one hand and cut with the other—this saves half the effort. These shears are also used for cutting roots.

The long-handled shears #2 and #102 are used for thinner branches or for trimming off fine roots. Because of their handles, they are also good for cutting off branches in the center of the tree.

The other two shears, #28 and #128, are used for the same purpose as the two above, although their main use is for cutting off branches in the center of the tree.

For trimming even larger branches, use root cutters #14, #15, or #40, which can also be used to shave the cut areas afterwards. Root cutter #138 can be used together with the other three to cut off branches in narrow places, while in areas with more space, use #338. This is used for branches that are too thick for the blades of #14, #15, or #40.

After using the above-mentioned root cutters (#14, #15, #40, #138, #338), grafting knives or gravers will do the shaving work. When there are scars that are too big, binding agents should be painted on them to prevent them from drying up.

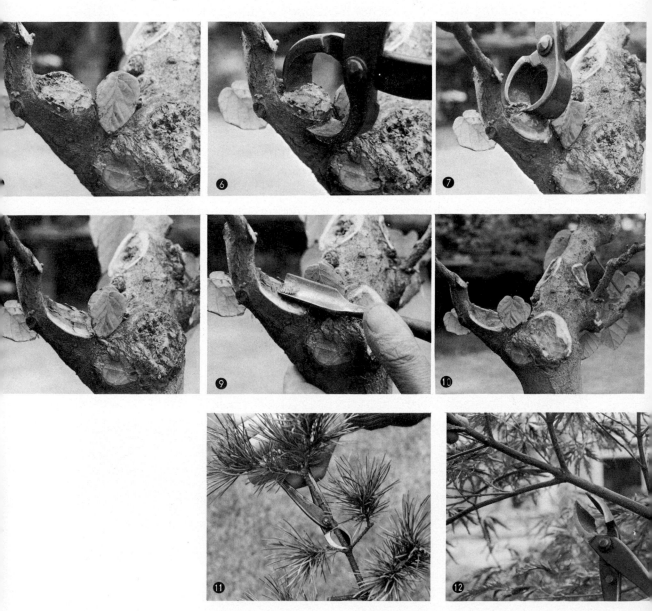

Root Cutters (1–3)

In the chapter on "Repotting" (pages 61–69), I have explained the necessity of cutting roots before the bonsai is potted or repotted. Use only sharp shears because if the shears are blunt, the root may start to rot where it has been cut. Also make sure that no pebbles or sand particles are clinging to the roots since these objects may damage the shears.

Thin roots can be cut with shears #1 and #101, or the long-handled shears #2 or #102, or the medium-handled shears #28 or #128 (*1, 2*). Roots that are as thick as a pencil should be cut with knob cutters #35 or #36, and even thicker roots with #14, #15, or #40 (*3*). The cut roots should always face downward, and spread equally in all directions (*4*). If the roots are too long and too thick, then the branches will also grow too long, so while repotting it is advisable to trim the branches as well as the roots.

Another point to remember while trimming roots is that you can correct an unproportional root growth during repotting. Roots will grow longer and thicker when exposed to the sun, so remove the soil and moss from the fine roots and expose them to sunlight. At the same time cover the long roots with soil to prevent them from growing. This will help even out the root growth of your bonsai.

Sometimes you may have a bonsai without any roots on one side of the trunk. This can be rectified by forcing roots to grow, since no branches will develop where there are no roots. There is a simple operation to do this. Cut off the bark on the side of the trunk where there are no roots. The cut has to extend into the xylem in order for it to be effective. Then wrap the cut section with sphagnum moss and cover with soil to prevent drying. In a short while new roots will form. When these reach a length of 2 in., expose them to sunshine to further their growth until they match the thickness of the other roots.

If this method does not work, then you can try layering (*see* page 55), but be careful to layer as closely to the new roots as possible.

For most deciduous trees, you should shave off the bark and cut into the xylem in a band one-and-a-half times the trunk's circumference.

For pine trees you should wrap the cut section with wire, tightly enough to cut slightly into the bark. Then cover with sphagnum moss and soil to prevent drying.

When the new roots have spread out sufficiently, wait until the repotting season the following year and then cut off the old roots as close as possible to the new ones. The old roots have to be trimmed with shears #14, #15, or #40 at an acute angle from the trunk, as close to the new roots as possible. Repot the tree (5) when the new buds are beginning to sprout.

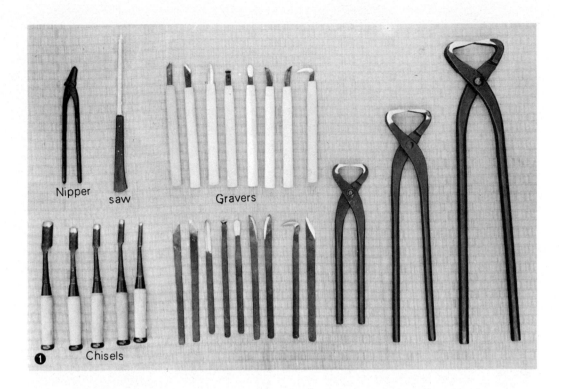

Nipper saw Gravers

Chisels

Tools for Jin (*1*)

These instruments are used to scrape and peel off bark from the trunk to produce *jin*, the bone-white, withered trunk that is used to add a supernatural touch to your bonsai. In Japan, *jin* is seen most frequently on Sargent junipers, pines, needle junipers, or *Ezo* spruces, while in America it is seen most frequently on the Californian juniper. In very old trees, when a branch or part of the trunk is withered, the branch or withered trunk can be left on the tree as *jin* (*2, 3*). This touch makes the tree more attractive, especially a young tree or a thick-trunked tree, like the needle juniper or Sargent juniper.

The tips of their branches can be made into *jin* by using nippers #17, and the slender saw #138, shears #113, #114, #115, and the chisel #39. Nippers #17 are used not only to peel off the bark but also to remove the tips of branches to simulate a natural break in order to produce *jin*.

The bark of a withered branch can easily be removed with these nippers by a simple up and down movement. The tip is pincered to the thicker part of the branch and the nippers are moved up and down to peel off the bark (*4–6*). This will not damage the woody part of the branch.

Another method is to cut the tip of the branch into a V-shape, trim the cut area with shears and smooth it with chisels and gravers so that the branch will not revert to its original shape (*7–13*). *Jin* can come in any shape from the simple to the intricate, just as it is found in nature.

Gravers and chisels can also be used to smooth cuts made on large branches or any large tree (*14–16*). The blades on the gravers are shaped so that they meet all the necessary requirements of carving and shaping. One point to remember when making a *jin* on a Sargent juniper: do *not* damage the red-colored vascular bundle inside the branch (*17*).

Tweezers (1)

These are very valuable tools in removing weeds from bonsai pots (2). Weeds invariably grow in the pot and sometimes they cannot be uprooted by hand. Tweezers are useful too in removing spiders and webs from the tree. Other uses are in spreading moss evenly (3), boring holes for cuttings, removing dried leaves, especially of the pine, the Sargent juniper, and the needle juniper. The spatulate area of the tweezers can be used to flatten earth after repotting (4) as well as to remove liverwort (5). The curved tweezers #27 and #127 can be used instead of a rake to loosen the soil when repotting miniature bonsai (6).

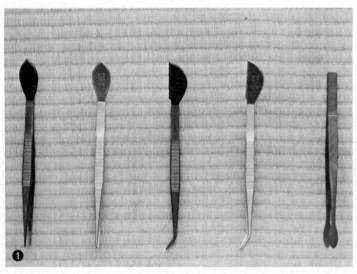

100

Levers and Jacks (7)

When trunks and branches are too large to be bent by hand, levers can make the work much simpler. If the bark of the trunk or branch is delicate, you have to protect it with raffia and wrap the lever in cloth. In most cases wires alone will suffice.

Adjust the length of the hook by turning the nut attached to it. If you push the handle of the lever to the right and left you will be able to bend the branch in any direction you desire. The angle of the curvature can be fixed by the position of the lever when clamped to the branch.

When you wish to straighten the branch, the reverse should be done. Sometimes there are other branches in the way and it is impossible to attach the lever to the branch. In such cases you should use two levers, one above and one below, or one to the right and one to the left of the branch. There are many positions when you are using two levers, and I think the best way to discover them is through experimentation.

When the branch is bent to the correct shape, remove the lever (or levers) and wire the branch so as not to allow it to assume its old shape.

Trunks with a diameter of more than 2 in. cannot be shaped with levers, so a jack is another useful instrument. The jack #23 is used for trunks with a maximum diameter of $3\frac{1}{2}$ in., and #24 is used for those with a minimum diameter of $2\frac{1}{2}$ in.

Aside from these tools there is a cudgel, #13, for removing insects and for scraping off scale insects. This is not an essential tool unless you spot insects on your trees. (8).

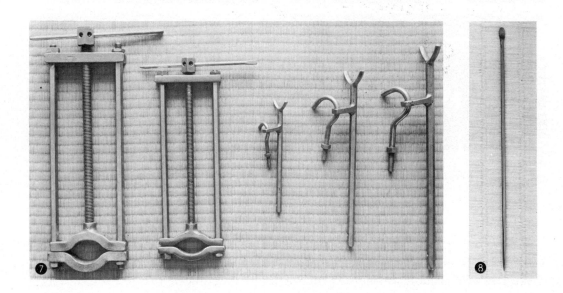

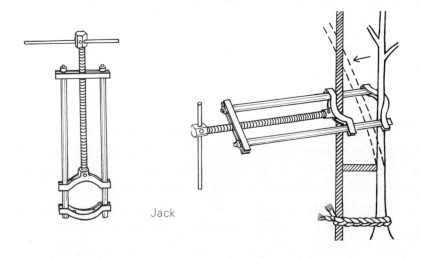

Jack

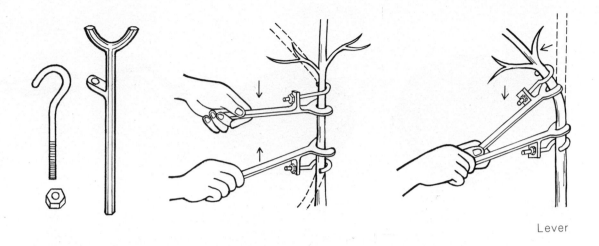

Lever

List of Tools for the Beginner

It is not necessary for the beginner to have in his possession all the tools mentioned above, but the following ones are most important.

> Sieve #900
> Bud-trimming shears, #3, #5 or #103, #28
> Leaf-trimming shears, #6 or #106
> Branch-pruning shears, #1, #2 or #28, #16, #216 or #116
> Root cutters, either #14, #15, or #40
> Wire cutters, #7, #8, #9 or #108
> Nippers, #18
> Turntable, #11, #29 or #30 (*9*)
> Tweezers, #11, #111 or #27 or #127
> Rake, #341
> Nozzle, #1010 (*10*)
> Sickle for repotting, #37

Apart from these tools there is a set of tools shown in the photo on page 104. This set, #33, is made up of five tools and is primarily for beginners. Other sets shown in the picture (*11*) are: a seven-piece set, #132, for miniature bonsai, an eight-piece set, #32, for the advanced bonsai enthusiast, and a nine-piece set, #31, for making *jin*. I advise you to start with these sets and gradually add to them as you become more skilled in the art.

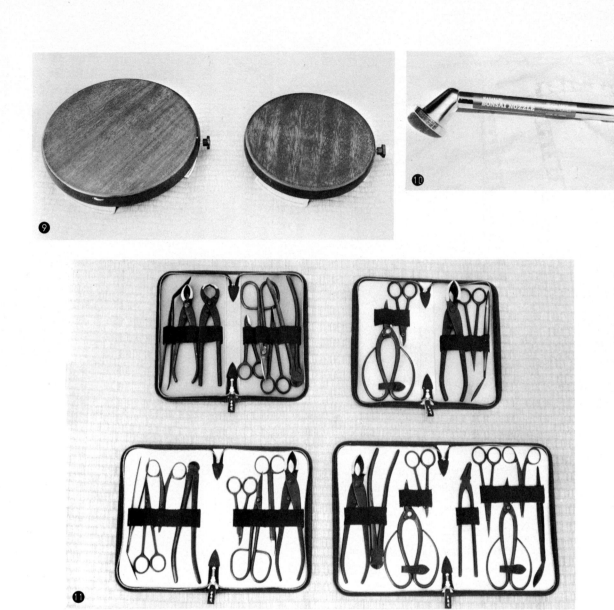

How to Care for your Tools

Rust is the greatest enemy of your bonsai tools. Even slight rust which cannot be seen by the naked eye will blunt the cutting edge of the tool, so it is important to clean your instruments immediately after use. Make this a habit when you buy your tools. Wipe with a clean, dry cloth to get rid of the sap, soil, and moisture. Pay particular attention to the reverse side of the blades and clean it thoroughly. To remove spots caused by sap, breathe on the blades and wipe clean. For more stubborn spots use benzene on the cleaning cloth.

When the instrument has been wiped clean, soak another piece of cloth in oil—any kind will do as long as it is mineral oil—and wipe the instrument with it. Do not forget to oil the joints when you do this. This easy method will prevent them from rusting for many years.

When the blades are blunt due to rust or to pieces falling off the cutting edges, sharpen them in the following way. For ordinary shears #1 and #2, spread the blades and place the surface of one blade on an oilstone. While you are sharpening you must not change the original angle of the blade.

Use an oilstone of rather coarse grain to remove rust first, then finish with a finer grained oilstone. Gasoline is the best type of oil to use on the stone.

You must never sharpen the back sides of the shears. When you have ground the surface of the blades, open and close the blades several times. The work is now completed.

If the width of the blades is more or less the same from top to bottom, as in #3, #4, #5, #28, #103, sharpen them when they are closed in the same way as mentioned above.

When a relatively large piece of the cutting edge has fallen off, repair the blade with a grinder, then grind it with oilstone, in the above-mentioned way. When using the grinder, take care not to let the blades become discolored by the heat generated during this process. The steel of the part that discolors will become soft and useless. To prevent this from happening, sprinkle water occasionally on the blades while grinding.

There are some shears (#16, #116, #316, #14, #15, #35, #36, #40, #113, #114, #115) whose upper and lower blades are metagnathous. In such cases, grind only the upper blade with the shears shut, and do not grind the lower blade. The lower blade will contact the upper blade when the shears are functioning and thus a cutting edge will be naturally formed.

In order to make the cutting edges last longer, you must first remove all sand or small bits of stone attached to the material you cut. This will prevent the blades from becoming blunt through use. Care for your tools will make them serve you long and efficiently.

CHAPTER 5

ROCK-GROWN AND MINIATURE BONSAI

It is the desire of every bonsai enthusiast to possess bonsai cultivated on rock or large stones, which resemble trees clinging onto high cliffs or plants growing on an uninhabited island. You can almost hear the wind and the waves rushing through.

It is not difficult to create these magnificent bonsai in any of the five styles given below, but before you do this, I would like to explain about the kinds of rocks suited to this purpose. The best rock is either volcanic or riverbed rock found throughout the United States. In Japan we use large stones that contain a large quantity of lime because lime erodes easily and this gives the stone an interesting appearance.

DIFFERENT STYLES OF ROCK-GROWN BONSAI

Formal Upright
The tree is planted on an upright rock. It goes without saying that a curiously shaped rock with interesting hollows would be best.

Waterfall
The tree is planted on a piece of rock which has white streaks flowing down from top to bottom. The branches of the tree will cover the streaks and this makes the whole effect quite stunning, as though the tree is growing in a deep valley. It has a cool look even during the hot summer months.

Flat Landscape
Trees are planted (as in the group style of bonsai) on rather flat stones, which can be either boat-shaped, islet-shaped, or with puddles that resemble lakes.

Boat-shaped
One of the most popular shapes of stone for rock-grown bonsai.

Stone Steps
This is an intermediate style between the upright style and the flat landscape style of rock-grown bonsai and resembles stone steps.

These styles, with the exception of the flat landscape, are all cultivated in a water basin, but there are also rock-grown bonsai cultivated in pots, where the roots crawl over the rock. The trident maple is the most suitable for this since its roots are strong and grow quite fast. The rock selected should be hard, since a soft rock may crack when the roots start to dig into it.

Species of Trees Suitable for Rock-grown Bonsai

Of the following species, the most suitable are:

a) Pine: The safest species to use.

b) Spruce: This will undoutedly be the most favored of trees in the United States, for the needles are short and the shape of the branches is sufficiently gnarled so that it will look like an old tree when it is grown on rock.

c) Sargent Juniper: Since this is a species which likes alkali it should be grown on rock high in calcareous content, like that found in Colorado.

d) American Cypress: This species is attractive and suitable for growing on rock.

e) Cedar: Choose a tree with small needles.

f) Needle Juniper: Its thick roots make it an excellent specimen for rock-grown bonsai.

g) Japanese Maple: Choose one with small leaves.

h) Trident Maple: This is the most suitable of the rock-grown variety for planting in a pot, as mentioned earlier. It is a strong tree and if the buds are trimmed regularly, the leaves will become small and uniform.

One word of caution about this style of bonsai. When you have selected a tree for this purpose, plant it in a deep pot, large enough not to have to repot for at least two years to ensure that the roots are thick and strong by then.

How to Plant a Rock-grown Bonsai from a 3-year-old Cedar Cutting (1)

1. First you will need to have all the materials in front of you—a turntable, wires (gage #20), instant binding agent, shears, nippers, vinyl or stainless steel mesh, a flat landscape stone with puddles (2), peat, and garden soil (3).

2. Screen the garden soil to remove the larger particles and mix eight parts of peat with two parts of soil. Add water and knead the mixture into small round balls (4).

3. Cut the wire into 8 in. lengths. Bend each wire in two, and adhere the bent section to the stone with instant binding agent (5).

4. Wash the roots of the trees thoroughly. I have chosen five three-year-old cedars of differing heights, one small quince and one azalea to plant underneath the cedars. The quince and azalea are last year's cuttings (6).

5. After washing off all the soil clinging to the roots, trim the longer roots and place the trees in water (7).

6. Place the round balls of planting soil on the stone (*8*). Keep the wires in an upright position (*9*), taking care not to bury them with soil.

7. Spread the roots out evenly and position them on the stone, as if you were pasting them on it (*10*). In doing this, be careful not to damage the small roots (*11*).

8. Hold these roots in place with the thin wires. Perform this very carefully in order not to damage them.

9. For extra protection against the wires, cover the fine roots with a soft material, like a piece of rubber or vinyl (*12*).

10. Cover the roots with soil (*13*). Place the vinyl or stainless steel mesh at the sides of the stone, fixing it with wire, so that soil does not spill over (*14*).

11. Spread a layer of moss over the soil and hold it in place with wire loops (*15*).

12. Water the tree thoroughly. Put some stones and pebbles in the water tray and fill it with water (*16*). Care for it in the same way as an ordinary bonsai.

Growing a Trident Maple in a Pot

For rock-grown bonsai you should select from five- or six-year-old trees (and one- or two-year-old trees if you are using miniature bonsai). The bonsai should be planted in a deep pot so that the roots will grow long and thick. At the annual repotting session, raise the roots a little to check if they will spread over the stone when planted on it.

When the roots have reached the required thickness you can plant them on the stone. As I have mentioned before, choose a hard stone with rough contours which run as vertically as possible. When the stone and the bonsai are matched, you can pot the tree in the same way as repotting bonsai (*see* Chapter 3). Place the roots in the crevices of the stone and plant the rest of the roots into the pot.

You may use wire, if necessary, to anchor the roots to the crevices of the stone, since the roots do not grow into them naturally. When the two have grown together, remove the wires, usually after three to six months. When the roots in the soil of the pot begin to protrude, you must cover them with sphagnum moss to protect them.

If you want your tree to grow quickly it is advisable to plant the bonsai in the garden and give it fertilizers to encourage growth, and then replant it on rock in a pot. When growing bonsai in the garden, trim the branches often and see to it that the branches do not get too thick. In other words, trim the buds regularly. Aftercare in this case is exactly the same as in ordinary repotting.

MINIATURE BONSAI

The height of ordinary bonsai ranges from ten inches to thirty inches. Bonsai which are shorter than six inches are called miniature bonsai today, although they have been known by a variety of other names in the past.

Care and cultivation of these miniature bonsai is the same as for ordinary bonsai, except that they have to be watered more frequently because their pots are so tiny. Liquid fertilizer, administered with a syringe, is the most common form of fertilizers used. (Rape cake balls are too large to place on the soil).

The shape of these bonsai should be in accordance with the species of trees in order to bring out their best features. The places where they are kept is also the same as for ordinary bonsai, but you should take care that the soil does not freeze in the winter.

CHAPTER 8

DECORATING WITH BONSAI

DECORATING WITH BONSAI

Here are a few guidelines on where to place your bonsai outdoors. Choose a place which is not in the shade from morning to noon. It should be warm in winter and cool in summer, and should *not* be exposed to the afternoon sun. It should have good ventilation, but be sheltered from strong winds. The air there should be clean and not too dusty. Bonsai also benefit from evening dew. In general select a place in your garden where it is most convenient for you to water, fertilize, trim the buds, spray, and disinfest your trees.

Those who do not have large gardens may display their bonsai beside the front door or garden gate, near the window, along a pond, on the veranda or on the roof. These last two places are best for ventilation and sun. If you put bonsai beside a pond or pool of water, the water will reflect the sun on the underneath part of the leaves, as well as adding to the beauty of the tree.

Do not weaken your bonsai by lavishing too much attention on them. This advice is especially useful for those who have a lot of other work on their hands. A weak tree is susceptible to changes in weather or climate and to disease. Rather, train your bonsai to be sturdy, and it will withstand weather, disease, and even a shortage of water or fertilizer.

Bonsai, like all other plants, may be left outdoors in winter. And, except for tropical or subtropical trees, there is no need to build protective shelters for the trees during winter. In Kawaguchi where I live, just north of Tokyo, the temperature falls to 25 degrees F. and there may be around 6–8 in. of snow in the winter, but I leave my bonsai outdoors on shelves just as usual. If, however, your natural environment is much colder, then I would advise you to build shelters as shown in the photos.

As for decorating your home with bonsai, there are no two bonsai enthusiasts who share the same opinion. This is where individuality comes in. In Japan we have developed certain fixed rules that govern all aesthetics, including bonsai, but in America, where they do not conform with your culture, it is up to you to develop your own. I will help with a few pointers.

The stand is an essential part of a good bonsai display. For pines and other trees with upright trunks, a grand, formal stand can be used (*see* p. 19). For deciduous trees, a more ordinary stand is better. Remember always that the stand should be two-thirds the height of the tree. If the branches grow more profusely on the right side, place the bonsai on the stand slightly to the left, and the grass on the lower right. Reverse these positions if the branches grow on the left.

The grass used for display with the bonsai should set off the tree at the same time. For instance, when the tree looks majestic, the grass should look inconspicuous; when the tree looks dull, the grass should have characteristics that help to brighten up the tree.

In a Western-style room, the bonsai should be placed at eye-level when the person is standing. Nowadays there is a trend to put bonsai on shelves instead of stands. For miniature bonsai, place several of them on staggered shelves. Since the heights of the trees are different, put high-growing trees up high, and low-growing trees on lower shelves. If you have a hanging scroll, you can hang this beside the tree to give it a formal, Japanese touch.

Display your bonsai according to the season. In winter choose a tree that suggests warm weather, and in summer, one that suggests the cold. Bonsai may be placed indoors in an unheated room for a week, but only for two days in a heated room. In the spring bonsai can be put indoors for only two days, or for a week if it is taken outdoors every evening. The same is true in the summer.

For rock-grown bonsai, place it in a tray of water to make it more attractive. If you are using shelves, staggered shelves are best for an assorted display of bonsai. The best places for them outdoors is at the edge of a pool, on the veranda, or at the corner of your lawn.

Shelters for bonsai in the winter

APPENDICES

APPENDICES

ADDITIONAL NOTES TO THE COLOR PLATES

The bonsai trees shown on pages 29–32 have been photographed in the United States for this book by kind permission of the owners, with the height and age of the tree inserted in parenthesis where possible.

American East Coast Maple, courtesy of Mrs. Luther Young.
Collected American Crab Apple, courtesy of Mrs. Luther Young.
North American Alberta Spruce, courtesy of Mrs. Luther Young.
Pitch Pine, courtesy of Mrs. Luther Young.
Blaauw's Juniper, courtesy of Mrs. Luther Young.
Montezuma Cypress (46 in., 15 years old), courtesy of John Y. Naka.
American Hazelnut, courtesy of Mrs. Luther Young.
Swiss Mountain Pine, courtesy of Francis E. Howard.
Californian Juniper (41 in., 350 years old), courtesy of Richard Wydman.
Hollywood Juniper (40 in.), courtesy of George Yamaguchi.
Golden Cup Oak (14 in., 150 years old), courtesy of Ben Oki.
Pomegranate, courtesy of Brooklyn Botanical Gardens.
Prostrata Juniper (20 in., 30 years old), courtesy of Takenori Imagire.
Silver-Blue Atlas Cedar (*left*), courtesy of Brooklyn Botanical Gardens.
Silver-Blue Atlas Cedar (*right*), courtesy of Margaret Guiney.
Elm (16 in., 20 years old), courtesy of Kay Hamasaka.
Japanese Maple (18 in., 40 years old), courtesy of Dr. J. Tayson.
Black Pine (28 in., 100 years old), courtesy of Frank Nagata.
Ohia Lehua of Hawaii, courtesy of Haruo Kaneshiro.
Bougainvillea (37 in., 25 years old), courtesy of Kiyoko Hatanaka.

The bonsai styles shown on pages 33–36 are identified below with the names of the trees and their owners. The height and age of each tree is inserted in parenthesis.

Straight Trunk: Olive (49 in., 45 years old), courtesy of Ben Suzuki.
Slanting Trunk: Chinese Wistaria (30 in., 50 years old), courtesy of George Yamaguchi.
Multiple Trunk: Olive (22 in.), courtesy of Chuichi Kawahira.
Twin Trunk: *Pinus amabilis* Rehd., courtesy of Brooklyn Botanical Gardens.
Triple Trunk: *Juniperus chinensis*, courtesy of Brooklyn Botanical Gardens.
Sinuous Root: Prostrata Juniper (23 in., 20 years old), courtesy of Kiyoko Hatanaka.
Group (*left*): *Juniperus chinensis var.* Foemina (48 in., 30 years old), courtesy of Umenori Hatanaka.

Group (*right*): Prostrata Juniper (57 in., 23 years old), courtesy of Ben Suzuki. (This miniature forest consists of 51 trees.)

Cascading: Deodara Cedar (24 in., 25 years old), courtesy of Dr. Seymour Dayton.

Semi-cascading: *Ilex crenata*, courtesy of Brooklyn Botanical Gardens.

Twisted Trunk: Californian Juniper (33 in., trained 10 years), courtesy of John Y. Naka.

Patterned: Prostrata Juniper (24 in., 30 years old), courtesy of Mickey Mizutani.

"Literati" Patterned: Hollywood Juniper (8 in., 20 years old), courtesy of John Y. Naka.

Rock-grown: Wild Strawberries with *Atlanthus altissima*, belonging to the author.

Bonsai planted in rock cavities: *Juniperus procumbens* (15 in., 10 years old), courtesy of Fred Yoshimura.

Bonsai planted on exposed rock: Trident Maple (15 in., 34 years old), belonging to the author.

A LIST OF TREES AND SHRUBS

American bald cypress	*Taxodium distichum* Rich
American cypress	*Chamaecyparis thyoides* Britt.
American hazelnut	*Corylus americana* Marsh.
American juniper	*Juniperus chinensis var.* Foemina
Azalea	*Rhododendron sp.*
Beach pine	*Pinus contorta* Loud.
Beech	*Fagus grandifolia*
Blaauw's juniper	*Juniperus chinensis var.* Blaaui
Black spruce	*Picea brevifolia* Reck
Californian juniper	*Juniperus california* Carriere
Canadian hemlock	*Tsuga canadensis*
Canyon oak	*Quercus chrysolepis lobman*
Cherrystone juniper	*Juniperus monosperma*
Chinese elm	*Ulmus parvifolia* Jacq.
Collected American crab apple	*Malus sp.*
Common juniper	*Juniperus communis* L.
Douglas fir	*Pseudotsuga menziesi*
Ezo spruce	*Picea jezoensis* Carr.
Five-needle pine	*P. pentaphylla* Mayr. *var. Himekomatsu* Makino
Flowering quince	*Chaenomeles sinensis*
Golden cup oak	*Quercus charysolepis* Liebman
Japanese beech	*Fagus crenata* Blume
Japanese black pine	*P. thunbergii* Parl. *var. corticosa* Makino
Japanese cedar	*Cryptomeria japonica* D. Don
Japanese cypress	*Chamaecyparis obtusa* Endl.
Japanese hornbeam	*Carpinus laxiflora* Blume
Japanese larch	*Larix leptolepis* Gordon
Japanese maple	*Acer palmatum* Thunb. *var. Matsumurae* Makino
Japanese red pine	*Pinus densiflora* Sieb. et Zucc.

Loblolly pine	*Pinus taeda* L.
Lodgepole pine	*Pinus murrayana*
Long-leafed willow	*Acacia longifolia*
Long-needle pine	*Pinus longifolia* Roxb.
Montezuma cypress	*Taxodium mucronatum* Ten.
Mountain laurel	*Kalmia latifolia*
Mugo pine	*Pinus mugo Pumilio*
Needle juniper	*Juniperus rigida* S. et Z.
North American Alberta spruce	*Picea glauca var.* Albertinia
Norwegian spruce	*Picea abies* Cv.
Olive	*Olea europaea*
Pitch pine	*Pinus rigida* Mill
Pomegranate	*Punica granantum* L.
Prostrata juniper	*Juniperus squamata var. Prostrata*
Pyracantha	*Pyracantha augustifolia* Schneid.
Rhododendron	*Rhododendron Metternichi* Sieb. et Zucc.
Rock cotoneaster	*Cotoneaster horizontalis* Decne.
Sargent juniper	*Juniperus Sargentii* Takeda
Scarlet maple	*Acer rubrum* L.
Shore pine	*Pinus contorta* Loud.
Silver-blue Atlas cedar	*Cedrus atlantica var. Glauca*
Swiss mountain pine	*Pinus mugo Pumilio*
Trident maple	*Acer Buergerianum* Miq.
Utah juniper	*Juniperus osteosperma*
Wax tree	*Rhus succedanea* L.
Weeping willow	*Salix babylonica* L.
Wistaria	*Wisteria floribunda* Dc.
Zelkova	*Zelkova serrata* Makino

BONSAI CLUBS IN THE US

American Bonsai Society
Address: Box 358, Keene, New Hampshire 03431

Bonsai Clubs International
President: Wilma Swain
Address: P.O. Box 1115, Rosemead, California 91770

Bonsai Societies of Florida
President: C.G. Eschenberg, M.D.
Address: 579 Man O War Circle, Cantonment, Florida 32533

Bonsai Society of Greater New York Inc.
President: Hal Mahoney
Address: P.O. Box 14, Oakland Gardens, New York, New York 11364

California Bonsai Society
President: John Y. Naka
Address: P.O. Box 78211, Los Angeles, California 90016

International Bonsai Arboretum
Director: William Valavanis
Address: 412 Pinnacle Rd., Rochester, New York 14623

Potomac Bonsai Association
President: Bill Merritt
Address: C/o US National Arboretum, 24th & R St., N.E., Washington, D.C. 20002

INDEX

jack, 73, 101, 102
Japanese beech, 47
Japanese black pine, 24, 25, 26, 47, 54
Japanese cedar, 25, 51, 54
Japanese cypress, 25, 51
Japanese hornbeam, 47
Japanese larch, 25
Japanese maple, 24, 51, 54, 61–64, 90, 110
Japanese pots, 41
Japanese red pine, 26
jin, 26, 97–98
juniper, 24, 25, 26, 54, 57 (*see also* individual species: American, Californian, cherrystone, *Itoigawa*, needle, Sargent, Utah, wild)

knob cutter, 75, 93, 95

layering, 47, 54–56, 96
leaf trimming, 63, 69
—shears, 90, 103
lever, 73, 101, 102
liverwort, 38, 100
"loathsome" branches, 91–93
loblolly pine, 23
lodgepole pine, 24, 57
long-leafed willow, 23
long-needle pine, 24, 57

maple, 25, 26, 27, 57
marigolds, 61
minerals, 27
miniature bonsai, 113, 114, 118
Montezuma cypress, 23
moss, 38, 95, 96, 100, 112, 114
—sowing, 40
—species of, 38, 54
—transferring, 38–39
mountain laurel, 57
Mugo pine, 24, 57, 75

needle juniper, 93, 97, 100, 110
New Brunswick, 57
nippers, 64, 73, 97, 103
North American Alberta spruce, 23
Norwegian spruce, 23
nozzle, 27, 38, 39, 50
nurseries, 37, 41, 47

Ohio, 57
oilstone, 105

parent and child bonsai, 25
patterned bonsai, 25, 42, 43, 75
peat, 49, 110
pine, 42, 54, 57, 69, 91, 97, 100, 110 (*see also* individual species: beach, five-needle, Japanese black, Japanese red, Japanese white, loblolly, lodgepole, long-needle, Mugo, pitch, shore, Swiss mountain)
pitch pine, 23, 56
planting bonsai, 47–58
—by grafting, 47
—by layering, 47, 54
—from cuttings, 47, 49, 58
—from seeds, 47, 58
—from nursery stock, 47, 57
—from wild trees, 47, 56
—position in pot, 43
pomegranate, 24, 51, 54
porcelain pots, 41
pots, 37, 41, 62
—selecting, 42
potting, 47, 51
—rock-grown bonsai, 113
—time for, 47
prostrata juniper, 24
purlite, 49
pyracantha, 24

raffia, 101

raft bonsai, 25
rainwater, 27
rake, 48, 62, 103
rape cake, 81, 82, 114
red maple, 23
repotting, 27, 28, 43, 55, 61, 63, 69, 96
   —Japanese maple, 61–64
   —other species, 69
rhododendron, 57
rock cotoneaster, 24, 50, 51
rock-grown bonsai, 26, 109–114, 118
root cutters, 47, 94, 95, 103
root distribution, 48, 54, 56, 57, 95
rust, 104

Sargent juniper, 24, 93, 97, 98, 100, 110
saw, 97
scarlet maple, 23
scissors, 50, 62
seedlings, 47
semi-cascading bonsai, 26, 42
shaping bonsai, 73
shears, 74, 89, 90, 93, 95, 96, 97, 103,
   105, 110
shelters for bonsai, 117
shelves for bonsai, 117, 118
shore pine, 23, 57
shovel, 38, 40
sickle, 62, 103
sieve, 40, 47, 48, 50, 87, 103
sieve scoop, 87
silver-blue Atlas cedar, 24
single trunk bonsai, 51
sinuous root bonsai, 25
slanting trunk bonsai, 25, 42, 49
soil, 28, 37, 38, 47, 48, 49, 57, 62, 63,
   110
   —screening, 47
soil bucket, 50
sphagnum moss, 54, 95, 96
spliced graft, 52, 54

sprinkling can, 27
spruce, 26, 93, 110
stand for bonsai, 117
straight trunk bonsai, 25, 49
styles of bonsai, 24–26
sunlight, 28
Swiss mountain pine, 24

tap water, 28
Temperate Zones, 23
Texas, 23, 57
threadworm, 61
tools for bonsai, 87–105
trident maple, 63, 64, 90, 110, 113
trimming shears, 74
triple trunk bonsai, 25, 51
trowel, 38, 39, 40, 48
turntable, 62, 73, 75, 103, 110
tweezers, 38, 39, 40, 73, 77, 100, 103
twin trunk bonsai, 25, 51
twisted trunk bonsai, 26

University of California, 37
upright bonsai (straight trunk bonsai),
   75
Utah juniper, 56

vermiculite, 49
vinyl mesh, 47, 50, 62, 110, 112
vinyl tape, 53, 54, 56
Virginia, 23

watering, 27, 38, 39, 50, 63
   —with fumigator, 40
wax tree, 47
weeping willow, 51
well water, 27
"white mold," 69
wire, 50, 62, 101, 110, 111, 114
   —annealed copper, 74
   —copper-colored aluminum, 74

ACKNOWLEDGMENTS

The author wishes to thank the following organizations in the United States for their invaluable help in the preparation of this book.

The Californian Bonsai Society
The American Bonsai Society
The Bonsai Clubs International
The International Bonsai Digest

He would also like to express his appreciation to the following persons in Japan who have assisted him with guidance and advice.

Mr. Teisuke Takahashi
Mr. Kyūzō Murata
Mr. Norio Murata
Miss Machiko Kon
Mrs. Mary M. Lockwood
Mr. Hirokuni Kawasumi